To

_____

From

_____

Date

_____

BUILDING GREAT RELATIONSHIPS

OMOBA'BINRIN ADEOLA OSIDEKO

BUILDING GREAT RELATIONSHIPS

Copyright © 2018 by **Omoba'binrin Adeola Osideko**
ISBN: 978-1-944652-81-4

Printed in the United States of America. All rights reserved solely by the publisher. This book or parts thereof may not be reproduced in any form, stored in a retrieval system, or transmitted in any form by any means - electronic, mechanical, photocopy.

Published By:
Cornerstone Publishing
A division of Cornerstone Creativity Group LLC
Info@thecornerstonepublishers.com
www.thecornerstonepublishers.com

Author's Information
To contact the author or to order copies of the book, please: email: omobabinrinadeola@gmail.com
whatsapp: +2348171999660

FOREWORD

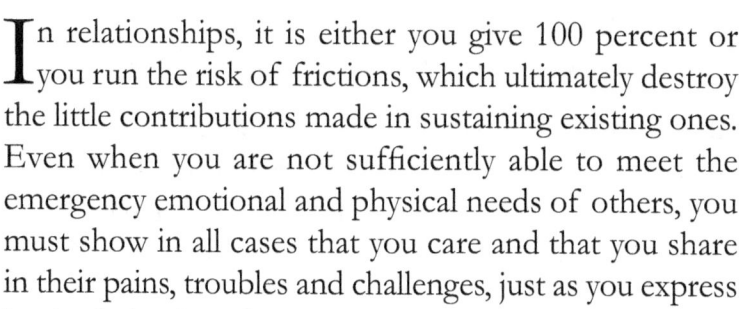

In relationships, it is either you give 100 percent or you run the risk of frictions, which ultimately destroy the little contributions made in sustaining existing ones. Even when you are not sufficiently able to meet the emergency emotional and physical needs of others, you must show in all cases that you care and that you share in their pains, troubles and challenges, just as you express joy in their triumphs.

The quality of connections among the various units, individuals and households in a community is sufficient in determining the quality of life of the people. Therefore, the benefits of building and sustaining good relationships are unquantifiable and cannot be overemphasized

We all do a lot of things on daily basis. In fact, we do some without a deep understanding of why we do them or how well they should be done. These little things are important to maintaining healthy relationships with people around us and, in this book, more light is shed on the various behavioral issues we have in our society.

Adeola, whom I have come to know as a young friend

and successful chartered accountant shows the attributes of positive social and individual relationships succinctly in this book. I am not surprised as this book comes from a lady sired by a well-known clergyman in Remo land, Ogun State of Nigeria, Late Reverend Felix Adedoyin Adesipe. The book adequately brings to fore the most needed prerequisite for human success, which is relationship-building between and among spouses, friends, colleagues, acquaintances and so forth. This, I dare say, is the secret to a progressive society.

In this book, you will understand more about building successful relationships with people in your environment and how to maintain those relationships. So many issues are discussed, such as trust and respect, maintaining healthy integrity status in our relationships, emotional intelligence, self-esteem, how to handle criticisms (especially the negative ones) and so on - all of which will lead to living a successful life as an individual in a dynamic society.

I highly recommend this book to all those who want to make a success of their families, businesses and social endeavors - particularly youths who seek for a feel of the past to enable them chart a glorious future.

Happy reading!

Olusegun Dada

Chairman, Nigerian Association of Small Scale Industrialists, Ogun State Chapter.

DEDICATION

To my late dad, **Rev. Canon Felix Adedoyin Adesipe,** and to all young people out there who are striving to become better each day.

ACKNOWLEDGMENTS

I want to thank God for the grace to write this piece. It had been a lot of efforts, resilience and self-encouragement, which finally made my dream come true.

I want to specially thank my husband for his ceaseless efforts in motivating and inspiring me to write this great piece. Ademi, thank you for your resilience in making this great dream a reality. I owe you a lot.

To my children, thanks for giving mommy space while working on this book.

I want to thank Mr. Olusegun Dada for taking time out of his busy schedule to read and digest this book for correction and for writing the Foreword. Many thanks to friends and family who motivated and inspired me to put this great piece together. God bless you all.

Many thanks to the publisher for doing a good job on this publication.

CONTENTS

Foreword..5

Dedication..7

Acknowledgments...8

Introduction..11

Chapter 1
What is Relationship?..17

Chapter 2
Communication Etiquette..................................41

Chapter 3
Money Matters in Relationships........................59

Chapter 4
Relationship Management.................................71

Chapter 5
Building Trust in Relationships........................85

Chapter 6
Handling Criticism..93

Chapter 7
Self-Love, Self-Esteem and Self-Confidence............101

Chapter 8
A Brief Insight Into Emotional Intelligence (EQ).........115

Chapter 9
The Magic Words...133

Chapter 10
Living a Successful Life.......................................143

References..153

About the Author..155

INTRODUCTION

In this book, we will be talking about relationship management, which is how to build and maintain long-lasting relationships with people in our environment. Relationships are key to our lives, as nobody can live in isolation. We need people to survive, and a study has found that social isolation can increase one's risk of having a stroke or coronary artery disease by as much as 30 percent. While the study was observational, it suggests that addressing loneliness could play a major role in tackling the two major causes of death in wealthy societies.

Friends and family are very important in our lives. They are like oxygen when we want to reach the summit of any mountain. They stand by us in our challenges, on our miserable days. When the whole world misunderstands us, they whisper in our ears that we can do it, that we can achieve it and that everything is going to be fine.

Some people are so poor because all they have is money. There is more to life than money and there is more to life than what money can buy. If you want to truly know how rich you are, drop a tear and see how many hands come forth to wipe that tear. Our happiness is not in our increased standard of life or in things but in people, in relationships. It is this meaningful, heartfelt, deep bonding of love that brings fulfillment to the heart. It is those meaningful exchanges of love that we share with each other in relationships that bring true joy to the heart. And isn't it the greatest irony that something that brings the greatest fulfillment is such that we can very conveniently neglect?

Friendship and family relationships are the most powerful leveraging tools in the world. They are the vehicles the rich use in getting richer and they are also what the poor use in getting poorer. In Africa, especially where we have a good social system and not everyone minding their business, friends constitute wealth. It's only a bad businessperson that will abandon old friends because he found new ones. Most of us have friends but we are not maximizing the potential of our friendships.

What does it mean to have a friend? Why do people need friends? As humans, we cannot live without interaction. We cannot live without being loved or without love. We need people who can understand us; we need people who can support us through our ups and downs, our hormonal changes, our mood swings. Humans, no doubt are the most highly evolved of all creatures and so we just cannot roam around wearing nothing - we need clothes. We cannot just pick fruits from trees and satisfy our hunger; and just drinking water from any nearby source won't help to quench our thirst. We need a system to live and so we need friends and family.

Friends become increasingly important to health and happiness as people age, according to new research in the Personal Relationships journal. They're so crucial, in fact, that having supportive friendships in old age was found to be a stronger predictor of well-being than having strong family connections.

A recent paper explored the findings of two studies about relationships. In the first, involving more than 270,000 people in nearly 100 countries, author, William Chopik, found that both family and friends relationships were associated with better health and happiness overall. But at advanced ages, the link remained only for people who reported strong friendships.

Family is important, to be sure; and by family I don't necessarily mean the group of people with whom you share the greatest genetic similarity. I mean that core group of people who really help define and frame who you are. Those that see you warts and all, and accept you and care for you and act in your best interest (sometimes even in spite of yourself) and help you when you need it. Those people who know what you are capable of, and do what they can to nurture the best in you. Those people who really do want you to be the best you that you possibly can.

Friends are equally important. By friends, I don't mean people with whom you are on a first name basis; people with whom you are cordial and with whom you don't experience great personal or professional conflict; or people with whom you eat pizza and drink beer. I mean the people who, while not actively trying to nurture and care for you and think of you and grieve with you and celebrate with you, generally add more happiness to your life than they cause sorrow. I mean people who take the edge off of the hard times by reminding you that there are good people out there, and even though you are not an integral part of their lives, or they a part of yours, you can make the world just a little more pleasant with your interactions.

As much as friends and family are great to have, you can be more independent and self-sufficient when you keep getting people in your life who are not what you want or need. This will make you to understand the place of self-esteem, self-confidence and self-love. Loving yourself first supersedes all kinds of warmth and affection you may receive from family and friends. It's extremely unlikely that without the ability to love oneself a person can ever be happy. In other words, what's necessary and sufficient—not for loving another but for a state of inner contentment and well-being—is healthy self-love and acceptance. For it only makes sense that if you're not on very good terms with yourself, you're not going to be happy with life generally.

I've seen many individuals who are quite capable of caring deeply for others but struggle mightily to extend this same care toward themselves. They'd regularly reveal profound misgivings about who, deep down, they believe they are. These and many other issues are what this book will enlighten us all about - how to take charge of yourself, control your emotions and relate well with people in your environment because this has a lot to do with you living a successful life.

CHAPTER 1
WHAT IS RELATIONSHIP?

Relationship is defined as when a person or thing is linked or associated with something else, or people with whom one has social or professional contact or to whom one is related - especially those with influence and able to offer one help.

So, relationship is more than DATING (romantic relationship); it cuts across all areas of life - family, friends, work colleagues, neighbors, business associates/ partners and so on. And how well we can manage all these relationships has a lot to say about our living a successful life.

An interpersonal relationship is a strong, deep, or close association or acquaintance between two or more people. It may range in duration, from brief to enduring. This association may be based on inference, love, solidarity, regular business interactions, or some other type of social commitment.

Interpersonal relationships are formed in the contexts of social, cultural and other influences. The context can vary from family or kinship relations, friendship, marriage, relations with associates, work, clubs, neighborhoods, and places of worship. Such relationships may be regulated by law, custom, or mutual agreement, and are the basis of social groups and society as a whole.

Why do you think interpersonal relationship is important to our lives? The truth is, throughout our lifetime, we must relate with people whether we like it or not. From the cradle to the grave, we need people! No one can live in isolation, as healthy human relationships are a vital component of our health and wellness.

Conversely, the health risks from being alone or isolated are comparable to the risks of smoking cigarette, high blood pressure, obesity and any other health disorder we might think of. Isn't it amazing that being alone for a long time is as bad for your health as smoking 15 cigarettes a day!

Research has shown that healthy relationships can help you live longer, deal with stress, be healthier, be happier, richer, and free from depression and anxiety.

In this book, we will be discussing some basic human

relations tips and rules that can help you develop more positive relationships in all areas of life. In developing sound relationships, there are some key things we have to understand. The most important ingredient in the formula of success is knowing how to get along with people because it determines how far we will go in life.

Understanding human relations is the most profound experience we can have in our lives. The connection we have with other human beings, when positive and supportive, will help us to feel healthier and happier; and mostly, we will get more satisfied with our lives.

We have various types of relationships, which vary from blood/family relations to friendship, to work colleagues, to neighbors, to school/classmates, to boss and superior, to mentor and mentee. As we grow in life, we come across a lot of people - from our school days to work days to married days - and it is important for us to be able to manage all our relationships with these people well because it says a lot about our personality, how the external world perceives us and how we perceive ourselves.

Human relationship is the relationship with or between people and particularly how we treat people. It is also the connection we have with other people.

As young children growing up, we are amidst people that we call family. We begin our journey of life from there. We begin to recognize them as we grow up, and based on the understanding we have about them, a connection and bond is developed and this makes the care, love and affection they show to us have an impact on our lives.

The relationship we have with our own father or mother can be very close, or just close, or not close, depending on the family we find ourselves and the situation on ground. Some are even close to their extended family than their immediate family; it all depends.

Apart from our family, we also meet a lot of people in life that we establish connections with and some of these relationships are key to our success stories.

I can remember the kind of strong likeness I had for one of my teachers then, just because he was very good at what he does and he is very diligent. This made me very passionate about the subject he taught us then.

However, it is very necessary to be able to identify the place of all these relationships we have with people in our lives and be able to manage them well.

I will be talking about family, friendship and some other relationships that we all have as humans, how to manage these relationships well, and how to improve our standard of life with them.

Note that you cannot manage all relationships the same way because each of them has its own peculiarity and there is a need to identify with that. Relationships can be broadly divided into the following three categories:

- Family

- Friends

- Romantic relationship

We have other relationships outside these three broad categories: workplace relationships (colleagues, superior, boss), acquaintances and so forth. However, this book will be focusing majorly on family and friendship.

FAMILY

"Family is not an important thing, it's everything" —Michael J.Fox

Family consists of a group of people related by blood (this is the simplest definition you can get). Family can also be through connection by marriage or adoption. "Family" includes your siblings, children, spouses and parents, as well as relatives who you may or may not be interacting with every day, such as your cousins, aunts, uncles, grandparents, and stepparents.

Typically when we think of families, the traditional nuclear and extended family who are biologically related may come to mind. However, a family can include anyone that a person considers to be their family. A family shares emotional bonds, common values, goals and responsibilities. Family members contribute significantly to the wellbeing of each other.

In most societies, the family is the principal institution for the socialization of children, in terms of internalizing morals, norms and ideologies of the society. Humans need social experiences to learn their culture and to survive. The family is essential for the whole process of learning throughout the life course and is a central influence on the behaviors, beliefs, and actions of adults, as well as of children.

Positive family relationships are associated with children's emotional and physiological responses to stress supports, while negative family relationships and experiences are associated with such a wide range of negative outcomes for children.

We believe most times that family is more important than friends because of the blood connection that is involved and that they will always love us, regardless of what, even when every other person rejects us. We first learn about loving and caring relationships from our families. Ideally, each child is nurtured, respected, and grows up to care for others and develop strong and healthy relationships. This does not mean that it is always easy to make or keep friends; it just means that we share the goal of having strong relationships.

FAMILY RELATIONSHIP

Having healthy relationships with your family members is both important and difficult. Many times, however, families become blocked in their relationships by hurt, anger, mistrust, and confusion. These emotions are natural and normal, and only few families do not have at least a few experiences with them.

Children thrive on the feelings of belonging and affection that come from having caring and supportive families. Research affirms that the quality of family relationships is more important for children's wellbeing than the size or composition of the family. Whether families have one parent or two, whether they include step-parents, grandparents or guardians, they can build strong, positive family relationships that promote family wellbeing and support children's mental health.

Every family is different and made up of different people, with different needs, ideas and ways of behaving. This can make a family a special group. But it can also mean that getting on well with each other isn't always easy.

It is never too late to begin the process of improving family relationships – even if they are already of good quality – by developing some simple skills that we will be discussing in this book

Whereas in other situations you can step back and assess the relationship, it is often hard to do this with your family. Your family may have a constant presence in your life; so when an argument or issue arises, it may seem impossible to handle.

Remember that communication is key to resolving conflicts. While it may seem that your siblings are constantly present to annoy you or boss you around, they are also there to communicate. Meanwhile, talking to your parents is a really important step in having a good relationship, and talking can make a difficult relationship better. This can help you connect more and make your relationship a little bit easier. It may also help your parents feel that they can be there for you when you go through difficult times.

Sometimes it's easier to talk about the little things. You could start by telling them something about your day, or asking them how their day was.

Use your family's presence to your advantage – communicate with each other, develop ways to value boundaries, and build trust and respect.

SEEK HELP

If you are feeling unhappy or are being hurt by someone in your family especially, it's important you get support as soon as possible.

- If you always seem argue too much;
- If you feel unsafe or threatened;
- If your family is trying to force you into a marriage;

- If your parents have drugs problems or going through divorce or separation;
- If you are neglected or not being looked after;
- If you don't get on well with your step family.

DEVELOPING HEALTHY FAMILY RELATIONSHIPS

Over the past 20 years of my life, many things have changed, including my friends, styles, morals and jobs. With everything constantly changing around me, there is one thing that has always stayed the same: my family.

When I think about my happiest moments of life, they all involve my family. My relationship with my parents, husband, children and siblings is something that I learn to treasure more and more every day. There are many important things in life, but the most important thing to me is family.

My family has made me who I am today. Without my mom pushing me to excel in school and encouraging me to take some jobs that I felt were not worth it, or my husband forcing me to develop my public speaking career, I would not be where I am today. They have challenged me, loved me and made me a better person. They have guided me through life and have constantly been my number one fans. There has never been a moment in my life when my family was not there when I needed them. They have been there with me through my best times, worst times and times where I did not think I had anyone.

The older I get, the more I come to the realization that people who say they will always be there for you are not always there for you. But whether it is 2 o'clock in the morning or 4'oclock in the afternoon, I know I can always count on my family to be there for me.

If I ever need a good laugh or cry, I know I can always go to my husband. He is not only my family but also my best friend, soul mate, and partner in crime. He knows how to give the best advice and he is always positive and smiling. Whenever I am having a bad day, I know I can count on him to brighten my mood or calm me down. He is truly one of the most beautiful people in the world, and his happiness gives me life.

Whenever I am stressed out or need advice, I can always go to my mom. She knows when I am stressed and need a reality check or when I am proud and need humbling. She has gotten me through the toughest times in my life and has made some of the best moments in my life possible. Without her, my life would be less colorful.

Even my children, as little as they are, they are a spar of joy that keeps me going. They are so much concerned about me and how I am faring, especially my little daughter, and they make my burden lighter with their smiles any time they are around me.

My dad would have been my superhero if he was alive. He was strong, intelligent, and sincere. He knew how to give the best advice and be the better person.

My siblings are equally awesome. They are the ones I can turn to when I'm in a tight corner. Their support and love have kept me stronger.

The keys to developing healthy family relationships are not farfetched. They include: making relationships a priority, communicating effectively and providing support for each other.

Happy families work together to make decisions and ensure that each family member's needs are being adequately met.

Spend quality time with your family. Yes, it is good to work. But in-between that your tight and busy schedule, find time for your family. Spending time with children is more important than spending money on them. Go for affordable vacations, picnics, excursions, and dinners. Make sure you also participate actively in family parties and gatherings. Stop giving the excuse of "I am busy". Everyone else too is busy; they just take their family important and take out time to attend.

After a while, you will no longer live together and you will be all scattered all over the places for survival. Try to keep in touch with one another, through calls, texts, chats or visits, especially your aged parents; do not just abandon them without checking on them. Studies have shown that it can increase their life span by keeping them happy and healthy.

Remember one other's birthdays or any other special anniversaries. You can even plan surprises for those dates.

You need to understand that families are different. They vary in the expectations they hold regarding children's behavior and the roles of parents. Cultural background can influence the values and goals adults have for children's development. Many beliefs about what makes for strong family relationships are influenced by the values and experiences that parents were exposed to in their own families while growing up; so do not compare your family with another family. There are so many things that could have caused the difference.

If you want to build lifelong, loyal friendships; if you want to build trust, learn to protect your family members and friends, even when they make mistakes. Don't make your family a subject of mockery, no matter what. When you sell them cheap, you are not placing value on yourself either.

When everything is going well in your life, you will have many people by your side to share your happiness and to support you. But when you are going through a bad phase, many of those who stood by your side in your good phase will abandon you. You will be alone and will have to face all the problems by yourself. That's when you realize that you are not alone, even in tough times. You will have a few people who will stand by your side, no matter what - and that's family.

Your family will be ready to support you, no matter what, and help you to get through your tough times. Well, the only problem with us is, we often don't realize all this, until something we can never forget happens. So, love your family and know their importance, right from this moment. Spare time for them and spend time with them.

Never forget the power of family. Make sure to thank your parents every day. Call your siblings to see how they are, and cherish every moment you have with them. Without them, you would not be who you are today. Family is the best and most important gift in our lives, and it is important to embrace it every day.

Without each member of my family celebrating with me, crying with me, laughing with me and grieving with me, my life would simply not be the same. I would have no one to call all day long, no one to run to, no one to share my accomplishments with, and most importantly, no one to love unconditionally.

FRIENDSHIP AND FRIENDS

Life will definitely be boring without friends. Yet, friends are hard to discover and it's even more challenging to find great friends!

The old adage says it all: "A man is known by the company he keeps." It is very important for our wellbeing to be a great friend to someone and to have a group of good friends supporting you. It can be hard to pinpoint exactly what makes a good friend. Friends will come and go in your life, but more important than how long a friendship lasts is that a good friend will love you for who you are.

Friendship is a relationship of mutual affection with people. Friendship is a stronger form of interpersonal bond than an association. Although there are different types of friendship, there are some common features they all share such as kindness, love, mutual understanding, loyalty, sympathy, empathy, honesty, as well as freedom to be oneself and express one's feelings without the fear of judgment from the friend.

There are different types of friends. We have intimate friends, casual friends, work pals, talking friends, course mates and so on. Some are very intimate, while others are just pals.

One thing is key here: choose your friends and never allow them to choose you. Your friends are like buttons on an elevator - some take you up while others let you down; choose wisely!

How you relate with each class of friends is different; the level of intimacy you maintain with them is different. Some might be so close to you that you can hardly do things without informing them. They are like the next to you.

Managing friendship is a lot of work and, just like every other relationship, there is tendency for conflict and misunderstanding because of the level of closeness. Research has shown that intelligent people have fewer friends than the average person. In other words, the smarter a person is, the more selective they are.

Yes, you do not have a choice of family as you just open your eyes and find yourself in one; but you do have a choice in the kind of people you allow in your life as your friends

While choosing your friends:

- Ensure your personal beliefs and values agree with theirs. You cannot hang out with negative people and expect to live a positive life.

- Make friends with people whose strength is your weakness; they will help you overcome it.

- Friendship is actually a decision; do not let anybody force themselves on you.

- Do not be quick to make people your friends because of their status, position, fame or riches.

- Let relevant things be your drive to the friendship.

- Choose quality over quantity, you don't need to have lots of friends just choose the best ones

Below are some tips that you will find helpful in your friendship:

1. When you finally make your friendship choices, try to be friendly in that relationship. Be genuine, be kind, be loyal, and remember: to be liked, you have to like. Portray good manners and don't be rude in conveying your ideas. Good manners are not only needed at the workplace and other professional settings, they are also important in friendship and our other day-to-day dealings with people. After all, we do have some friends who are older than we are - don't they deserve some respect, despite being friends with us?

2. Do not treat friendship as a favor. All relationships are mutual; so do not see your friendship to the other person as a favor and start behaving as if you are the best and the other person will not survive without you. And do not expect too much from any friendship because too much of expectation kills relationships

3. Do not breach confidentiality. Be a secret keeper.

No one likes their secret kept with you to be all over the place. Learn to keep your friend's secret. If you need to tell someone else for any reason, try and seek your friend's consent. Confidentiality is an essential part of any healthy relationship. Consistent communication in relationships can only occur when both parties feel comfortable enough to share their innermost selves with each other. In all relationships, any confidential information that is shared must be guarded like a treasure.

4. Accept and celebrate differences. Do not force your opinion on your friends. Personalities differ, and you need to understand that. That is why it is important you are friends with people who share same or similar school of thought with you. With this, passing your message across to them or expressing your opinion about certain things will be easier.

5. Set a boundary. You meet someone on the bus today and the next few days you have started sharing intimate stuffs with them; that is too fast! Apart from the length of time you have known each other, there are things that are better shared with family than friends. They both have their different roles and places in your life. The most important thing is that you talk to somebody about some issues you may be going through during your rough times - but maybe not your friends. Sometimes, a counselor or your parent or spouse may be better.

Boundaries are the limits we set for ourselves as individuals in relationships. They protect our sense of personal identity and help guard against being overwhelmed by the demands of others. Boundaries also help signal to others how we want to be treated, and prevent us from feeling used, spread too thin, or being in desperate need of defending ourselves.

In life, we all have got layers. Some are near the surface; you don't mind people seeing them. But there are some deeper layers that you don't just share with anyone.

6. Know boundaries and respect them. All relationships have boundaries, regardless of how intimate the relationship is. It's just that some boundaries are wider than others, depending on the level of intimacy. Learn to respect people's boundaries and space. They will only let you know what they feel you should know. Boundaries are healthy and they're about the kind of respect a person thinks they deserve.

7. Listen more during conversations. Do not ignore or sleep while your friend is talking to you. If you are feeling sleepy or the conversation is no longer interesting or convenient to your timing, politely excuse yourself, rather than making the other person look stupid.

8. Think about what you can give to them. Remember your friends' special dates such as birthdays, wedding

anniversaries, children's birthdays and any other special times and celebrate them. Give compliments when you see anything good on them or when they have done well in any area.

9. Respect space. Nothing kills friendship faster than suffocation. Give your friends some space when they need it. Do not pick offence when your friends want to spend some time alone or with other people. Do not be too friendly unnecessarily. Allow them have some time to themselves if they so wish.

10. Be yourself. Do not try to impress your friends or oppress them. Drop the mask and do not try to be someone you are not. You will lose respect the day you are finally unmasked. Be truthful and honest. Dishonesty will cause trust issues and may eventually break the friendship bond.

11. Be kind with your words. You can be generous with words of praise, warm greetings, sympathy, love or other good news. Be careful with your choice of words, some words are too indecent to use for your friends and such might irritate them. Nicknames can be funny but be sure they are the ones that do not cut straight into their ego because ego has no sense of humor. Watch your friend's reaction when you are picking nicknames and some other words you use for them and be sure they are comfortable with such.

12. Call your friends by their names. There is nothing

more interesting to us than our own names. Show that you remember the other person's name. This act goes a long way not only in friendship but in other relationships. It gives a person a sense of belonging. A person's name does not just have power, it has far more power than most people can readily imagine. Try and learn names fast when you meet people; it shows you are genuinely interested in them. And do not make it obvious to them when you have forgotten their names. If you do, it can be very embarrassing. Try and find a means of covering up.

Also note, don't not try to shorten people's names except they give you permission to do so, or you see other people calling them the shortened form of their names and you think they are comfortable with it. Some do not like it and they may consider it offensive, while some don't mind. For me, I prefer people calling me "Adeola" to "Deola". Of course, I don't take offence, but I prefer my name pronounced in full; it makes me feel good.

13. Do not be too proud to say sorry. Learn to apologize to your friends when you are wrong. Apology doesn't mean you are weak, it only shows how mature you are to have realized you have hurt someone and to pledge to do better henceforth.

14. Demonstrate personal integrity. No one wants to be friends with liars and dishonest people. Maintain a

good image with your friends; be truthful and be straightforward. Do not withhold their change when asked to buy things for them – yeah, it all starts from there! A friend is an asset that can get you to your desired place in life, but your good image will determine how well that will be.

15. Do not make promises you cannot fulfill in the name of being supportive or showing off. Yes, there are times the failure to meet up may be due to circumstances beyond your power, but if you have not been doing that before it will be understandable. When we don't keep a promise to someone, it communicates to that person that we don't value them and that we have chosen to put something else ahead of our commitment. Even when we break small promises, others learn that they cannot count on us and it also shows we don't value our own words. Not keeping a promise is the same as disrespecting yourself. Ultimately, it can harm our self-image, self-esteem, and our life.

16. Learn from their mistakes. Nobody is perfect, even your friends. It is certain that in their lives, they must have made certain mistakes and as true friends with a lot of life experience, they will give you pieces of advice that are guided by their experience so that you do not make the same mistakes.

17. Invest your energy more on your good friends. Do not forget that good friends still exist, don't carry the mindset that friends are bad or allow your past experience with your bad friends rip you off the benefits you can get from the good ones. Let them know you appreciate and value them

18. Stay away from bad friends. The Signs of a Fake Friend Aren't Always Obvious

Sometimes it is very clear that a person doesn't have your best interests at heart, and sometimes a disingenuous person will subtly display their true feelings. Unfortunately, we live in the kind of world where we'll run into these kinds of people. Don't take it personally when you encounter a fake friend. A person who is fake to you will also be fake to others. It is likely that this fake person doesn't have any real friends at all, and you're no exception to that. When you notice a fake friend just walk away because it can be detrimental to your life.

The below points will help you identify a fake friend:

- when the friendship is conditional

- When your friend acts differently when you're around other people

- Fake friends will speak poorly of you when you're not around

- Fake friends will stop talking to you when you have a disagreement
- Fake friends disappear when someone "more interesting" shows up
- Fake friends always seem to want something from you
- Fake friends will stop hanging out with you if you say "no" to them
- Fake friends never try to help you achieve your goals
- Fake friends always bring you down
- Fake friends don't listen to you
- A fake friend sees your needs and wants as a nuisance
- Fake friends don't accept you for who you are

The biggest sign that you have a fake friend is that your friendship is extremely conditional. we all have normal boundaries that we don't want people to cross, but conditions are totally different boundaries are healthy and they're about the kind of respect a person thinks they deserve.

What DO YOU DO when you notice a fake friend? WALK AWAY! It is not everybody that you loose is a lose

CHAPTER 2
COMMUNICATION ETIQUETTE

Communication is simply the act of transferring information from one person/place to another. It is the process by which information is exchanged between individuals through a common system of symbols, signs, or behaviors. We have verbal, non-verbal and written forms of communication.

Communication is one of the most important human attributes. It is the process of encoding a message and sending it to another individual or group, using a specific medium.

What makes human beings different from animals? It is the way they carry themselves in the society. Here comes the importance of manners and etiquette. It is essential for an individual to behave in a responsible manner acceptable to the society. People around us must not feel embarrassed by our behavior. One should not behave irrationally or illogically in public.

WHAT IS ETIQUETTE?

Etiquette is simply defined as good behavior, which distinguishes human beings from animals. Human beings are social animals and it is really important for us to behave in an appropriate way. Etiquette refers to behaving in a socially responsible way.

According to the Oxford dictionary, etiquette is the conventional rules of personal behavior in polite society. It is about being well-mannered, courteous and showing respect for others.

As individuals, we simply need to be conscious of the subliminal harm we may do unwittingly through communication and modify our behavior accordingly

NEED FOR ETIQUETTE

- Etiquette makes you a cultured individual who leaves his mark wherever he goes.
- Etiquette teaches you the way to talk, walk and, most importantly, behave in the society.
- Etiquette is essential for an everlasting first impression. The way you interact with your superiors, parents,

fellow workers and friends speak a lot about your personality and upbringing.

- Etiquette enables the individual to earn respect and appreciation in the society. No one would like talking to a person who does not know how to speak or behave in the society.

- Etiquette inculcates a feeling of trust and loyalty in individuals. One becomes more responsible and mature. Etiquette helps individuals to value relationships.

There are different forms of etiquette, namely: social etiquette, corporate/professional etiquette, meeting/interview etiquette, eating/dining etiquette, clothing/dressing etiquette, communication/telephone etiquette, business etiquette etc. In this book, we will be considering only communication etiquette. In the subsequent edition, we will consider other forms of etiquette.

Contrary to the belief that communication etiquette is mostly needed in the professional world, it is actually more needed in the outside world so that it becomes a part of us and we do not have to start learning hard when we are in the professional world. Good manners are not inherited from generation to generation; they are learned skills that become part of us in the long run.

First impression, they say, lasts longer. We meet new people from time to time - at conferences, on the plane, at gatherings, at parties, at the workplace, during networking events, in classrooms, at church, mosque and so on. It is not only first impression that lasts longer, continuous impression also does; so there is a need for us to keep our day-to-day relationship with people up to standard, so that we can create an enabling environment for ourselves in the workplace and in the society at large.

The first five minutes of conversing with a new person can give you a little insight into who the person is, and having some communication etiquette is a good way of setting your path straight for those few minutes. After all - nobody knows – some, you will never see again, and some will become friends, colleagues or partners with you for years.

Communication etiquette is not only useful for new relationships, it is also very good if it is continually maintained for existing relationships. And in today's workplace, your communication etiquette is constantly being observed. People are getting an impression of you, often without you even realizing it. Every part of your communications—technological (texting, email, social media), verbal and body language—must send a message of professionalism and good manners.

There is no single set of rules that constitutes good communication etiquette. Communication is personal and relies so much on context but the points below will be helpful:

- Try, as much as you can, to avoid misunderstandings. It is impossible not to experience any form of misunderstanding in our relationship with people, day in day out. That is the way nature makes it. Different upbringing, coupled with different beliefs and values, is also a major cause. But in all these, learn how to communicate with others as clearly as you can; avoid misunderstandings, sadness and drama. Make your stand clear without being rude or saucy. Be aware of your tone and body language, because they speak louder than your voice.

- Practice mindful listening. Listening to others is a way of showing respect. So many people want to be heard and are not ready to listen to what others have to say. Always be cautious of your listening skills; do not interrupt while the other person has not finished his or her point. You might be missing something or jumping into a wrong conclusion if you are not calm enough to listen.

- Do not assume. Assumption is a deadly disease in communication. It causes confusion, problems, misunderstandings and unproductive conversation. Most of us are guilty of this. We make assumptions about what someone else is trying to say - because of speech patterns, tone of their voice, the way some people talk (some talk faster than others, while some use pauses in their conversation style) - and we end up misinterpreting what they said or what they are trying to say. We fail to realize that communication takes mindfulness and effort. Do not be lazy to ask questions when in doubt; rephrase what was said in your own words to get clarification as to what the speaker means.

- Body language. Body language goes beyond words and says a lot, even when you have not opened your mouth to say anything, or while you are speaking. It consists of gestures, body movements and eye contact used in sharing how we feel, despite what we may be saying.

  Body language is a good way of showing how we feel. Sometimes we ask people "how are you?" and the popular response is "I am fine". Most times it's not everyone that is actually fine, but body language will help you figure out what the sincere response is and if you really care, you may want to ask further question to be sure the person is actually fine.

  But even at that, body language can still be misinterpreted; so you can always ask questions for clarity

- Be conscious of the setting (is it formal or informal?) Make use of your formal communication skills, while at work or any official gathering. Professionalism is core and it must be handled as such, especially during business events or in an official environment. Professional etiquette builds leadership, quality, business and careers.

This notwithstanding, it does not mean you should be too loose with your informal communication etiquette. Etiquette or manners expected in any group are the social rules that we live by in order to show respect to others, including ourselves.

- Respond in a timely manner. Communication is a two-way thing; every speaker wants a response, either in writing, verbally or even through body language. It shows them you are following and that they are not alone in the conversation. Return calls quickly. If someone leaves a message, call them back as soon as you can. This makes the other person feel important and makes them like and trust you more.

- Text messages or chat can be misinterpreted - because we may be reading them with our tone, rather than the intended tone of the sender. Most times, this causes confusion and anger. So, if you are not sure of the intended tone of the message, make a call, rather than replying angrily with a message again.

- Speak with kindness and caution. Before speaking to others, consider the potential impact of those words on them. Show empathy, pause and weigh those words carefully. Say them with softness, bearing in mind that a slip of tongue can inflict needless hurt. If you will criticize, let it be constructive and necessary.

- Do not shout or yell at people, no matter how small the person may be. There is a difference between talking loudly and raising your voice. You can make your voice clear and audible but make sure you are not shouting.

- Learn to greet first. I have seen people who do not greet - all they do is to just walk to you and table their request, or send chats to you without any word of greetings, even if they need your assistance in any form. It isn't bad if you say "Hello, good morning. How are your family doing?" or "Hi Adedapo, good afternoon. How are you today?"- before you start tabling your request. It is simple courtesy! Nobody likes to feel worthless. Greeting people means that you care about them more than that request of yours

- Learn to say "sorry", "please" and "thank you" (We will discuss this more in chapter 8

TELEPHONE ETIQUETTE

Telephone is an important device through which people separated by distance can easily interact and exchange their ideas. Got a brilliant idea and want to convey it to your friend staying out of the country? Use the telephone. Telephone is one of the easiest and cheapest modes of communication.

An individual needs to follow a set of rules and regulations while interacting with the other person over the phone. These constitute telephone etiquette. It is important to follow the basic telephone etiquette, as our voice plays a very important role in creating an impression of our personality, education, family background, as well as the kind of job we are engaged in. The person giving the information is called the sender and the second party is the recipient.

MANNERS REALLY DO MATTER

Always be polite, regardless of who is on the other end of the line. Whether you are talking to a receptionist or the company president or a friend or a relative, never forget to say "please" and "thank you". Aside from the fact that everyone deserves respect, the person who answers your call can make sure it gets dealt with appropriately.

- Always remember, your voice has to be very pleasant while interacting with the other person over the phone. Don't just start speaking. Before starting a conversation, use warm greetings like "good morning", "good evening" or "good afternoon", depending on the time. Smile through the phone. Keep a smile in your voice. Sound upbeat and enthusiastic about the chance to speak with the caller. Adults pay more attention to the tone of your voice than they do to the words you use. Remember to be sensitive to the tone of your voice. Do not sound overly aggressive or pushy. A polite word or two always helps in bringing warmth into the conversation.

While it is very important to take permission to speak to the person you have intended to call, one should always remember to use a polite tone. Use a phrase like "May I please speak with_____". It is important your tone conveys authority and confidence. Do not lean back in your chair when speaking on the telephone.

- Never call any person at odd hours like early in the morning or late night, as the person will definitely be sleeping and will not be interested in talking to you.

- In any official call, don't use words like "can you guess who I am?", as the person on the other side might be occupied with something and can get disturbed. You can say something like "Is it Tolani?", and do ask him, "Is it a good time to talk to you?" and then start communicating. If the person sounds busy, always wait for the appropriate time. After dialing, always reconfirm whether the person on the other side is the desired person whom you want to interact with. Always ask, "Am I speaking with Mike?" or "Is this Jenny?" before starting the conversation.

- Make sure your content is crisp and relevant. Don't play with words; come to the point directly and convey the information in a convincing manner. First prepare your content thoroughly and then only pick up the receiver to start interacting. The good old 7Cs of communication will always have an impact on how you converse with people. It is very important to remember and include the first "C", which is, being clear. Do not use broken phrases. Always use a clear, crisp and simple language. Always speak each and every word clearly. The person on the other hand can't see your expressions; so, remember, your tone should be apt to express your feelings in the correct form.

- Always carefully dial a number; never be in a rush or dial the number in the dark, as it can lead to a wrong call. If by mistake you have dialed a wrong number, don't just hang up; do say "sorry" and then end the call courteously.

- Never put the second party on a very long hold. Always keep the information handy and don't run for things in-between any call, as the listener is bound to get irritated.

- While interacting over the phone, don't chew anything or eat your food. First finish your food and then dial the number. If you are reading, please leave the book aside first; concentrate on what the other person wishes to convey and then continue with the book.

- After completing the conversation, don't just hang up. Reconfirm with the receiver whether he has downloaded the correct information or not and do end your conversation with pleasant words like "take care", "nice speaking with you" and a warm bye. Never say "goodbye".

- Don't take too long to pick up any call. If you miss the call, make sure you give a call back, as the other person may have an important message to convey. Avoid giving missed calls at the workplace, as it irritates the other person.

- In professional talks, never keep the conversation too long, as the other person might be busy. Always keep the content crisp and relevant and do come to the point after formal greetings. While speaking on phone, you are not in front of the other party; hence it is very important to ask if the receiver has enough time to speak with you. Respect the person's time and ensure that the conversation ends within the given timeline.

- If you are not the correct person and the speaker needs to speak to your fellow worker, always say "one moment please - I will call him in a minute". If the colleague is not in the office premises, always take a message on his behalf and don't forget to convey it to him when he is back.

- If you call once or twice and the person is not picking, take a break and call later. The person might be in the middle of something; they will always return your call when they are done. If it is something urgent, you can drop a chat or text message. If you leave a message and the person for whom you left it doesn't get back to you immediately, it may be because she can't at the moment. There is no need to call again and again. If it is a pressing matter, you can try calling again the next day or following up with an email stating that you also left a voicemail. Don't keep calling over and over again; it can be irritating.

- Swallow first. In other words, your mouth should be unoccupied when making a call or answering the phone. You want to be able to speak clearly and that is impossible if you are chewing or swallowing.

- Decrease the volume of the television or turn off the speakers while speaking over the phone, as noise acts as a hindrance to effective communication. Communicating over the telephone is much more effective when both parties can hear each other clearly without background noise.

Plan to make your call - whether it's for work or just to catch up with an old friend - at a time in which you are not required to attend to any other business, and ensure that there is no disturbance around. Blaring noises, such as the television or road traffic can interfere with your communication skills, making it difficult for a conversation. If there is any disturbance in the network, don't just keep speaking for the sake of it; try to call after some time with a better line.

- If I tell you some people in this age still use phone to "flash" rather than call (even when they are the one who need your help) won't you be surprised? It is funny but it's the truth. Do not flash someone for the purpose of them calling you back, except in the case of an emergency or danger. It is actually so annoying for me as a person. Why will you be flashing me for heaven's sake? If you want to call please do and if you know you don't have enough credit on your phone to call, that should be your own problem, not mine. Please, don't flash me to call you back. Personally, I find it insulting and rude whoever who you are.

I had almost finished writing this book when a vendor who was helping me work on something flashed me for me to call him back and I wondered why someone would do that. Did he think he was doing me a favor by rendering a service I paid for? I had to quickly add the experience to this book because I never knew such still existed. It had been a while that I last experienced or heard of it. Not even now that call card has been made affordable for all and sundry. Even if you don't have enough, you can still call and say, "Please, I do not have enough credit to finish this call, can you please call me back?" I think that is more polite and mature than flashing.

Remember, each of the above telephone etiquette must be practiced for an effective and healthy telephonic discussion and smooth flow of information.

THE USE OF ABBREVIATIONS

There is a trend of using abbreviations now in our society and so many people are abusing this practice. The introduction of social media has caused a lot of damage to the way most people now type. There's no denying that social media has transformed the way we interact with each other. From sharing our thoughts and photos to planning a night out, most people tend to organize their social lives, or at least have it significantly influenced by some form of technology-based engagement.

Social media has done a lot of good by enabling us to communicate with a much larger number of people on a global scale, in a way that we only really used to be able to do on a local level. This is great when it means we're keeping friendships alive over great distances; but it is also increasing the demands placed on individuals to keep a much larger number of relationships going simultaneously and this has increased the speed of communication.

The use of acronyms or emoticons to convey messages is also another feature of social media. However, this continues to affect speech and communication etiquette in the real world. Language is an evolving thing. It's naive to think that the language of social media isn't having an effect on the way we use English in day-to-day life. It's more appropriate to consider just how much of an effect it's having on the way we communicate. Many words originating from social media and the wider Internet have become so commonplace that they've now slipped into popular usage, and we don't realize it. Some are even carried away to the extent that they write official correspondence like memos and mails or prepare official document, with abbreviation, which is not acceptable.

Another curious phenomenon we've seen in recent years is the reappropriation of existing words, and words based on brands, to refer primarily to their social media context. Reappropriation is the cultural process by which a group claims words that were previously used in a certain way and gives them a new meaning. In this way, the people who engage with social media are quite literally creating new words and giving new meanings to existing words, such as unfriend, selfie and so on.

The attention of this topic is focused on the damage this new habit has done to our societal morals and values. Personally I find it insulting when a younger person or even my peer is chatting with me and using some abbreviations that I find disgusting. And, most times, you cannot even understand the meaning of these funny abbreviations. The question is, do I need to go through stress before I can understand what you are trying to pass across?

Communication should be concise and unambiguous and that makes the flow easy. Now that we have smartphones, typing is made easy because those words come out in full by the time you type two or three letters; it is sheer laziness to abbreviate. And come to think of it, what is the difference between "your" and "ur" - just a difference of two letters and I am not sure that will take a whole second to do.

THE HARMS OF ABBREVIATION

- It prevents you from learning new words.

- It has a lot to say about your personality and how people see you.

- It prevents you from speaking and writing correct words and you might get carried away with it.

- It can cost you a lot. I have seen someone lose a job because she typed a message full of abbreviations (that is even not understandable) to someone who was supposed to help her with the direction to the interview venue.

- It is not ideal for official settings, and even in relating with much older people. Maybe your friends and colleagues will understand, but it might pass a wrong message to other people.

In summary, abbreviation addiction is bad and we must try to reduce the extent to which we use it. It is not good communication etiquette

CHAPTER 3
MONEY MATTERS IN RELATIONSHIPS

Lending or borrowing money from family and friends is something most of us do. Money is a powerful instrument when it comes to relationship and lending money to family and friends is a generous act - and one that could easily backfire or even ruin your relationship. Shakespeare, in his words to his son, gave this timeless advice: "Do not lend money to friends." "But why shouldn't I lend money to a friend or family member?" the son asked. The reason is that it often results in the loss of both the money and the relationship and can in fact result in an entirely unexpected set of problems

It can be difficult to request repayment of a loan from a friend or family member. More than likely, the lender cares about the borrower, and doesn't want the borrower to feel awkward. The borrower may continue to worry about loan repayment, and thus shut down some or all communications with the borrower in order to avoid talking about the loan, while the lender becomes confused and hurt feelings can result.

When you borrow money from people who are close to you, remember that it is not that they have excess to spill out; they have just decided to be kind enough to ease your burden. So, be also kind enough to repay them as and when due. So many of us have misused the opportunity we have with various friends and family by borrowing money without paying back. We tend to take people for granted over their hard earned income.

It is equally important to know that it is more prestigious to keep a relationship away from borrowing, either from family or friends; and if need be, it should be a pressing need that is so important and should try and be repaid as and when promised. Some people abuse the generosity of others by borrowing money without repaying. This is a bad habit and has a lot to say about your integrity and personality.

Debts to loved ones are different from debts you owe to banks and other businesses. Banks don't mind if you take your time paying back your debt, as long as you're making, at least, the minimum payment on the debt, because that's what they're in business for. And remember, if you have borrowed from a bank it will be with interest. So, if your friend or family is kind enough to lend you money without interest, then be kind enough to make sure you repay.

But your friend is not a bank and likely does not find pleasure in serving as one; and because of their love for you, they can't take the same measures against nonpayment - for instance, sending debt collectors after you or ruining your credit. Show them the same love and be a better borrower to your friend than you would be to a bank.

Setting boundaries of clear and open communication between lender and borrower will help ensure that the transaction doesn't go wrong at any point during the loan period. Assumptions can be deadly: the lender might assume the money will be paid back quickly while the borrower thinks the money is, for all intents and purposes, a gift.

Lending money to friends or family can be risky if it all goes wrong. It's very hard to say no to a friend or family member in need, but you have to think about — and talk about — how and when the money will be repaid. If you can afford to give the money away, then make it clear that it's a gift; but if you expect it to be repaid, it's much better to discuss it upfront rather than after the event.

These are some of the reasons why people do not repay or like to repay money lent to them:

- Nonchalant attitude, due to too much familiarity.
- "He/she earns more than me, so they should be able to afford it even if I choose not to pay back."
- "He/she doesn't have children so they should have extra cash to loan out."
- "How much are we even talking about here? Just 10 USD or just 10,000 naira. That's not so much of money to die over."
- "He/she should be kind enough to understand my situation."
- "I cannot kill myself; I will only pay when I have it."
- "After all, he/she is rich; they should be able to forgo that little change' conveniently."
- They don't have as many responsibilities as I do."

THE LAW OF LENDING AND BORROWING

Dear borrower,

- Once you borrow money from a loved one, you change the dynamics and shift the power in the relationship. The borrower becomes the servant to the lender. Even though some lenders do not think that the borrower is less of a human being, but once there is a breach in repayment, self-value is lost.

- When you refuse to repay, you have only succeeded in blocking future opportunities to borrow again, even when the need is more pressing and urgent.

- Do not be too quick to borrow money for every need; it diminishes self-worth. Make sure they are really your NEEDS and not your WANTS. If you buy anything new, trust me, your lender-friend/relative will probably resent you for it. After all, if you can afford to buy new things, you should be able to repay your debt, right? Your loved ones might not come right out and say it, but yes, they do expect you to put off on purchasing those new shoes or that new computer until after you've settled your debt with them.

- Remember, the lender is giving you his/her hard earned income and deserves to be paid back. If someone who earns 100,000 per month gives you 5,000 out of his salary, it means he woke up for two days in the month, had his bath and went to work for you. Learn this simple arithmetic; it will help you to be grateful and repay.

- Money lent to you is not your right; it is only a privilege you are enjoying. Do not abuse this privilege by refusing to pay or seeing your prospective lender as your enemy because he or she says there is no money to lend you. I have seen someone blocked me on Facebook because she asked me to give (not even lend) her money - and this is someone I had given money to twice (not lend). Don't make anybody your enemy because they cannot meet your giving or borrowing needs. Nobody knows what tomorrow holds.

Remember, when someone says, "I don't have money", it means he/she did not budget for what you are asking for, not that they are broke. And it also boils down to learning to respect people's decision on their money, including who they choose to give or lend their money to. So do not have the mindset that they are rich and so should be able to give you by all cost

- One of the things you can do when you owe someone is not to avoid them, especially when you are finding it difficult to pay back. Owing money and not speaking about it makes your loved ones feel disrespected. Learn to speak up on the challenges you are facing in paying back, negotiate a new repayment plan and try to meet up with it

- Don't lie about what you want to use the money for in the first place. It will help you, especially when you have difficulty in paying back. Your friend can sense that you're not being completely honest or using excuses to buy more time and that makes your nonpayment even worse. If you're having serious financial trouble, come clean, and hope your lender will be merciful.

- Try and look at alternate ways of borrowing money. For instance, if you can get the loan from your workplace or a soft loan (in some companies) with little interest arrangement, so that it will be deducted from your salary/wages. With this, there won't be cause for defaulting or the embarrassment of borrowing from family or friend which may eventually not have a happy ending. And it will also save you from the heartache of them saying "no" to your request. Yes, so many people do not like the word "no"; it makes them feel bad. Even I hate that word. I would rather try to stay away from any scenario where that word can be avoided.

- Appreciate their kind gesture if someone has decided to lend you money; some are going the extra mile just to make sure you are fine. Do not say, "After all, I will pay her back - why should I say 'thank you'?" Remember, it is not your right, it is just a privilege!

- It is better to tell your family or friend to give you money as a kind of assistance than borrowing without repaying. If it's convenient for such friend, he or she will voluntarily give and none will be indebted to the other.

- Do not wait till you want to borrow money from your family or friend before you reach out to them. That attitude can put them off even if they can help.

Dear Lender,

As a lender, it is important you know that people have different attitudes toward money; so, do not compare your own attitude to money to what others' attitude to money looks like.

Before you lend people money, you need to consider this. "Can I forgo the money?" If your answer is YES, then you can go ahead and lend the person that money so that your mind is zero to either getting the money back or losing it; in this case, your friendship or relationship is still secure. But, if your answer to the above question is NO, then do not bother to give out that money, because it will eventually ruin that relationship you have just gotten or the one you have built for so many years.

Conventional wisdom holds that you should never lend more than you can afford to lose. Believe it! That is the principle I have been applying to my personal life, and sincerely, it has been working for me. I don't borrow people money I cannot forgo. From the day one I am giving the person, I have "zeroed" my mind that it is either I get it back or not. I always see it as a gift from the day one, rather than a loan and, honestly, this has saved me from lots of hypertension and heart attack I would have died of (smiling); and it has saved me from so many of my precious relationships that could have been ruined.

I do not joke with my relationship with people and I

try as much to preserve it. People who are close to me know that I don't easily give up on people, except the relationship is a threat to my peace of mind. So I do all I can to make sure I do not allow anything ruin my relationship with people.

Financial entanglements can ruin relationships. Here's what to do when a relative or friend hits you up for a loan.

- Even though you want to be a good person, and you want your friend or family member to love you, don't lend them money if you cannot help it. If a friend or family member asks for financial help, it can be really hard to refuse. But there's no point getting into difficulties yourself because you want to help, or because you feel bad about saying "no". You also don't want to lose a good friend or fall out with a family member because of money. Gently refuse the loan, and determine the best way to help your loved ones.

- Sometimes loving someone involves doing something that they do not want, and they may be disappointed or mad. But if you have their best interests in mind, it is easier knowing you won't jeopardize your relationship. If you can afford to loan money to a family member or friend, have an open and honest conversation to discuss any potential problems with the loan. Most of the time, issues related to these types of personal loans can be quickly resolved with a frank discussion.

- Remember, most borrowers have the tendency of coming back to borrow more after the first borrowing. Do not be surprised that even those who do not repay the first one may still come and borrow again. It is important to set the path right the first time. Ask yourself, "Can I tolerate this friend/family member enough to borrow them my money? Can I forgo the money if not paid? Can I entertain them again when they come back? Will this not ruin the relationship we share?" And remember, the more they come back to borrow, the higher the risk of not paying back, because by then they would have been so relaxed and nonchalance can set in.

- Also note that it can be difficult most times to ask for the money back. More likely the lender cares about the borrower and doesn't want the borrower to feel awkward; communication can be shut down and it often results in hurt feelings.

- Can you afford it? Take the time to work out your own budget before lending to anyone. Do not lend out money not meant for you or money you are keeping for your own need. Some people lend out money that another person kept with them with the mind that the borrower will return it. Please do not make such mistake; that is what is called "double wahala" in Nigeria. You cannot give what you don't have. And don't lend out money you are keeping for your child's school fees, your house rent or even your own exam fees. What if the money is not repaid? - because at times it is some situation beyond the borrower that won't make them meet up with the repayment.

- Try not to take advantage of the borrower in any form by subjecting them to ridicule or harassment in whatever form, just because they need your help at that time. Remember, nobody knows tomorrow and the table can turn at any time. If you need to say "no", say it politely. Do not insult or embarrass them. Some needs are actually genuine and pressing. If some of these "borrowers" have better choices, they wouldn't be coming to you. You can use words like: "That's not in my budget. Sorry." "I have a strict anti-lending rule: I've lost too many relationships this way." "I paid for your last car repair, and you haven't returned the money. I can't do it again. Sorry." "Let me look at my budget and see what's possible. I'll let you know by the end of the day tomorrow." (This is for when you're blindsided or it's an emotional situation. Go home and send a "that's not in my budget, sorry" email.).

- You can try to help in other ways. For instance, if your cousin or friend needs financial help on a regular basis, those cash infusions address the symptom rather than the disease. Whether it's careless spending or a lifestyle that's too big for them, the underlying issue needs to be fixed, not enabled. Offer help instead of a bailout. Suggest a wealth psychology expert who can call their attention to your observation (not to mock them but to help them).

- Can they afford it? Don't be embarrassed to encourage the would-be borrower to work out their budget as well. Be sure what they are borrowing is what you know they will be capable of paying back. It will be less awkward to do so before you lend them money than to find themselves in difficulties of repayment. You might be confident the person you've lent money to will be able to pay it back in full, but you still need to consider what you'll do if they can't.

- This is a deeply personal decision but one you should think about before handing over any cash, no matter how sure you're that they will repay you. Unless you're happy to give them the money, rather than lend it, you need to know that they will be able to pay back under the terms you agree.

CHAPTER 4
RELATIONSHIP MANAGEMENT

Who you associate with on a regular basis determines the circumstances of your life.

In a book titled "Your Habits Change Your Life", I found that one of the hallmarks of wealthy, successful people was their ability to somehow break free of the human tendency to unconsciously forge relationships with others. According to the "Rich Habits Research Interview", 177 self-made millionaires were interviewed over five years. Long before they became rich, the self-made rich people made an intentional, conscious effort to only forge relationships with individuals they aspired to be like: other rich and successful people.

The average person unconsciously chooses their friends, their boss, their spouse or their significant other. They unknowingly seek out individuals they feel comfortable with and then they wind up surrounding themselves with those similar people. Their associates all have similar habits, similar mental outlooks, a similar work ethic, and many other shared traits.

It's the "birds of a feather flock together" maxim. And, as I said, for the average individual, it's all happening unconsciously. The bottom line: Like attracts like. People with high-level formal education like to associate with the academic elite. Physically fit people enjoy spending time with others who are fit. Religious people like to have fellowship with people of faith. And rich people like to associate with others who are rich.

But, there's no need to blindly forge relationships that drag you down in life. You can choose those relationships that will lift you up. You can choose to be rich by choosing who you associate with. In order for you to know who to associate with, however, you must first know what to look for.

People who can help you create rich relationships have one or more of the following traits:

- Good habits
- Positive mental outlook
- Trustworthiness
- Encouraging attitude

- Fanatic loyalty
- Financial stability
- Hard work ethic
- Individual accountability
- Strong willpower and discipline
- Passion and enthusiasm
- Gratitude

Those are the traits you want to look for. But what about traits to avoid? People who tend to build toxic relationships tend to have the opposite characteristics of those listed above, such as like bad habits, a negative outlook, a victim mindset, and a tendency to blame others for things that go wrong.

When you become aware of the traits of these two disparate groups, it opens your eyes. You will begin to see the pluses and minuses in every individual you come into contact with, which makes it easier for you to decide which relationships to grow and which to avoid.

Rich relationships infect you with their good habits, positive mindset, and enthusiasm. They open closed doors for you. You will find your life's circumstances improve as you spend more time in them. So, relationships with people sometimes cannot be limited by age or social status or position. I have older friends and I have younger friends - it doesn't change anything. I have been opportune to move close to people who are rich and successful. However, it is important we manage our relationship well with these people so that its savor is preserved and maintained.

So many of our young generation do not know how to relate well with people who are not in their social class or age group. I guess they are carried away with the common friendship they are used to that doesn't require any extra effort or caution. Especially in this social media age when you can easily add a friend and someone can easily click on the add button to give you part access to their life and personality.

I have seen affluent people who are friends with middle class people, either by choice or coincidence; but most times, people do not treat such relationships with care because most of them feel they are doing a favor - "after all, we are not the same age or class". Let me say this to you that age or class should not be a barrier to a good relationship with people.

Do not treat a younger friend like you are doing them a favor. Our relationships with people should be mutual and any relationship that is not mutually beneficial should be avoided. One party should not see himself or herself as superior to the other.

Relationship with people who are not in the same class with you, either by age or social class, should be treated with respect. Allowing you access to their life is not a right (no matter how rich, poor. old or young you think they are) but a privilege; and so it is important you see it as one. Do not take anyone for granted. An inspirational quote by Wilson Mizner about the value of appreciation says, "Be nice to people on your way up because you may meet them on your way down."

These kinds of relationship are important because many people often climb the ladder of success fast through these kinds of relationship and it advised that you behave well. Age-gap friendships will help you to fit in any group of people, older or younger. You will learn a lot by spending time with the older and more experienced people. In their surroundings, you will get to know and experience many things in which you previously had no interests - for example, the old love quality music, much of which will help you in your business plans and the like. They are going to help you develop a more sophisticated taste of entertainment.

All this is important for you because in the company of people who are older than you, you will overcome that generational gap, and you will be able to communicate equally well with all age groups. Do you remember those uncomfortable situations where you were usually omitted from some topics of conversation, because of your age? They found that those were issues unknown to you. This will change.

Imagine that a single person to you can be a friend, a brother or sister, or a parent. It is also possible. Because someone who is older than you can put himself in all the situations that you're going through because they already went through same, and for that reason this kind of friend will understand you very well, and sometimes even better than your parents.

In most cases, your net worth mirrors the level of your closest friends. Is it time to start looking for some new friends? I'm not suggesting you go and "unfriend" all your friends just because they don't have a lot of money. And I'm not suggesting that you choose your friends based on how much money they have.

However, as Einstein said, consciousness is contagious.

If you want more money, you should consider spending time with/be a friend of people with more money. Exposure to people who are more successful than you are has the potential to expand your thinking and catapult your income. We become like the people we associate with, and that's why winners are attracted to winners. In other segments of society, this is accepted, but the rich have always been lambasted for their predisposition to engage the company of people with similar financial success.

But it is important that if you have access to these sets of people we have mentioned above, you don't abuse it. The following tips will guide you:

- Learn to greet before you start any conversation with them.

- Use their title alongside their names when talking to them, depending on their choice. At times you may ask "how do you want me to address you? 'Adeola' or 'Aunty' or how exactly?" Most times they will tell you which of it they prefer. For me, I prefer my younger friends calling me by name or simply 'Aunty'. I do not appreciate any unnecessary titles.

- Avoid the use of abbreviation; it can be so annoying even for your mates.

- You can use 'sir' or 'ma', depending on how they feel about it. You can ask as well.

- Be polite and courteous.

- Do not only check on them when you need their help. Once a while, drop a message to say "hello". Meanwhile, do not overburden them with unnecessary messages of "I just want to say hello", "how was your night?", "how was work today?" It's not bad to do all these, but keep it minimal. At times it can be irritating and disturbing their busy schedules.

- Avoid trying to borrow money from them, as much as you can. It passes the wrong message about your personality.

- Respect their privacy; do not ask unnecessary

questions or try to be unnecessarily concerned about them. Learn when to step back.

- If you need to share your personal stuff or anything with them, ask when if it will be convenient to call or chat them; do not just barge into them.

- Do more of call or text message than chat if the issues are important to you. Chats are more informal, except you are sure you have grown the relationship to that level.

- Know the various boundaries of the relationship and respect it.

- People like these appreciate gifts (even if it is little). From experience, it has been discovered that such people hardly receive gifts because the mentality is "they are rich", or "what can I buy that they will appreciate?" or "they would have already have enough of this". Try to get them a gift and watch how much they will appreciate it.

- Show them good gestures on their various anniversaries such as birthday, wedding anniversary, their children's birthday or graduation, house warming, new job appointment or remarkable promotions.

- Let them know you appreciate their presence in your life.

- Avoid eye service. Be real. Let them know the real you. If they can cope, they will still keep you around them; if not, they will move away from you. Do not try to be who you are not because you want to please them.

- Value the relationship and do not take it for granted.

- Present yourself well to them, dress well to their house or the events they have invited you to and do not be too loud.

- Respect their spouses as much as you respect them; nobody wants to see their spouses disrespected, even if they themselves disrespect them.

- Build trust and integrity. Keep to your word and follow through with your actions.

- To be honest with someone else, we must know ourselves. Make your actions match your words. Be sincere about your reactions. Having learned from experience, which is much larger than yours, these friends respect sincerity. It will never be a problem for them to talk openly with you about everything, particularly about what bothers them and all, with the intention that your relationship becomes good. Sincerity is, of course, what they expect in return.

Older friends aren't your parents; they are a simple step ahead of you, and so can give great advice on financial questions, dating/relationship, big purchases and so on.

Going to older friends before making a big decision may be insightful because they are more in their settled stage in life, which means their twenties were as wild as they should be and therefore they have plenty of lessons learned the hard way that they are more than willing to pass on to you before you even think about making the same mistakes.

In some more mature age, people think they already know everything, and that they have experienced and learned all. It is then that they meet someone older than themselves and realize that there is still a lot to go through and learn. And of course, the fact is that a man learns throughout life and older friends are there to remind them of it.

One of the major advantages of friendship with a person who is older than you is that through friendship with such a person you can also consider some things from an entirely different point of view - the one that you never took into consideration. Age usually shapes opinions, and you probably know how many times you have made a mistake in life's decisions because you did not consider things from a different point of view, all because of your immaturity and inexperience. Therefore, allow yourself to be exposed to the ideas of other generations because it is certain that just because of being a couple of years more than you, they have already experienced similar situations.

Honestly ask yourself: How many rich people are in your inner circle of associates and advisors? Set a goal in the New Year to double the amount of time you spend associating with people who are richer than you are. Doing so just might make you rich.

5 TESTS THE WEALTHY USE FOR PICKING NEW FRIENDS

1. Can you keep secrets? Many people have dirty laundry. Family secrets are known, but not talked about. One day you are told something juicy in the strictest confidence. You are cautioned not to tell anyone. Then they wait.

2. Criticizing family - When you interact with wealthy people, you often meet members of their family. They might make indiscreet remarks about their siblings' intelligence, poor dating choices, dress code or marital fidelity. Within their rules, family members can be critical of one another; outsiders cannot. When meeting the mentioned person socially, you should always be perfectly polite. When your wealthy friends speak badly about their family, you either don't join in or highlight a positive aspect about them.

3. Dining out - Although the wealthy might travel a lot, they have dinner together. People serving on charity boards might get together midweek with another couple sharing the same connection. Bills are either split evenly

or couples alternate paying. You either insist on paying half the bill or keep careful notes, so you know it's your turn to pay next time.

4. Being cheap - Here's a paradox. The wealthy love saving money but don't want anyone else to know that. It is like a hit on their ego. Especially if you are constantly talking about where to find something they've already bought at a lower price, or saying that you have already bought that same thing at a cheaper price somewhere else, they might feel belittled or seen as cheap which they don't want.

For example, if you know they love wine, and over dinner with some other people they are talking about a new find. They mention their favorite store and what they paid, and right there or later you approach them, mentioning a store you found that has the wine at a substantially lower price, it might sound to them that you are being cheap or that you are trying to downgrade them.

5. Follow-up - This is the most important test. In a conversation, you have mentioned a restaurant review, a new wine or a publication your firm just issued about the economy. The wealthy are really interested. You tell them you will get the information to them. The next morning you either e-mail or phone them. If it's a report, you mail it or drop it at their home. They will conclude that your excellent follow-up in your personal life is an

indicator of excellent follow-up in your professional life.

The reality is, millionaires think differently from the middle class about money, and there's much to be gained by being in their presence. Perhaps even more surprisingly, many millionaires are humble and don't view themselves as having "arrived."

The average person wants to meet a millionaire, so they can tell their friends they met a millionaire. Millionaires, on the other hand, want to associate with billionaires to learn how they think. One group is watching the game; the other is playing the game. The only question that matters: Which one are you?

The correlation between your friends and your level of wealth is one that is taught improperly from the start. Most parents never teach their kids about the importance of making contacts. They hope their kids are popular and make friends so they enjoy their days in school.

Wealthy parents have a different approach. Sure, they want their children to enjoy their years growing up, but they also know that building contacts, even as early as high school, can make the difference between a life of average success and one filled with uncommon opportunities. While most parents are hoping their kids become the best of the football team or the most popular cheerleader, the rich are concerned about building the child's social infrastructure for the future.

The message of associating with the wealthy often sounds elitist or discriminatory against the middle class. But it's not. It's nice to say everyone, regardless of financial status, has access to all the good things in life; but It's also naïve and untrue. Right or wrong, wealth offers privileges, and one of the most fundamental ways to start the wealth-generating process is to get around rich people and watch how they think. It's an eye-opening experience.

Relationship Management

In your own mind	Nonverbal signals	Staying in touch	Building trust
• Hold people in high regard • Assume the best • Wish them well • Choose to trust them	• Greetings • Healthy safe touch • Smiles from your heart • posture & proximity	• Regular check-ins • Provide updates • Initiate personal contact • Seek reciprocity	• Personal integrity • Reliability • Express positive emotions • Show interest, empathy & support

CHAPTER 5
BUILDING TRUST IN RELATIONSHIPS

Trust is a dusty concept these days, bordering on being old-fashioned. The concept means reliance on the character, ability, strength, or truth of someone or something. It means that you rely on someone else to do the right thing. You believe in the person's integrity and strength, to the extent that you're able to put yourself on the line, at some risk to yourself.

So often amidst the chaos of life and work, we forget the simple and powerful truth which is "trust". Most of us agree that trust is an essential foundation on which to build a relationship; yet, despite the great things we say about being honest—that it's "the best policy" or that "the truth shall set us free"—research tells us that we aren't so great at it.

One of the essential ingredients to build a great

relationship, a winning team or a culture of greatness is trust. Without trust, you can't have engaged relationships and without engaged relationships you won't be a successful person, leader, manager, salesperson, team member, principal, teacher, nurse, coach, etc.

Trust is essential to an effective team, because it provides a sense of safety. In the workplace, when team members feel safe with each other, they feel comfortable to open up, take appropriate risks, and expose vulnerabilities. Same with other relationships - when people trust you, it makes them feel safe with you; they will be comfortable to entrust their possessions, business or money in your hands, or even tell you their top secrets or things that are eating them up.

How can we create more trust when we continue to lie to the people closest to us in countless ways? Honesty is a key component of a healthy relationship, not only because it helps us avoid harmful breaches of trust, but because it allows us to live in reality instead of fantasy and to share this reality with another. Of course, every human being has his or her own unique perception of the world, but by sharing these perceptions with each other, we get to know each other for who we really are.

Trust is built over time, one interaction at a time, and yet it can be lost in a moment because of one poor decision. Admittedly, it's not easy to reverse ingrained mistrust; make the right decision.

HOW TO BUILD TRUST

The most valuable asset you can have is trust. It allows for flow and openness. When there is no trust, it becomes harder to get anything done. Think of one of your relationships where there is a lot of trust. Now think of another one with very little trust.

People who have trust issues cannot go far in life because everybody is afraid of dealing with them, as a client/customer, as a friend, as a business partner or as a work colleague.

Be honest. Honesty is the first and most important way of building trust. When we aren't open with our partner about what we feel and observe, we may grow cynical or start building a case against them that actually distorts and exaggerates their flaws. Be honest! My mother always told me to tell the truth. She would say, "If you lie to me then we can't be a strong family. So don't ever lie to me even if the news isn't good."

Living truthfully, things may not always have a fairy-tale ending, but as human beings, we are resilient. We can handle our partner feeling attracted to someone else; and we can handle telling him or her when we feel insecure, afraid, or even furious. We can handle pretty much anything, as long as we are willing to live in reality and face the truths that exist. Honesty in relationships makes us feel secure, because we know where we stand.

When we are honest with ourselves and people, we can experience the joy and excitement of having a real relationship, in which we are being chosen for who we are.

To be honest with someone else, we must know ourselves. We have to understand what we really think and feel about the world around us. Very often in life, we are either influenced by or conforming to a series of "what should be", imposed on us by society, particularly the culture within our family/country of origin. We may get married because everyone in our age is "settling down." Or we may refuse to get close to someone because our parents never got along well with them.

It's important to differentiate ourselves from harmful influences on our personality that don't reflect who we really are and what we really want. If a voice in our head is telling us not to take a chance or be vulnerable, it's important to question where those thoughts come from, then align our actions to that which we really desire.

When we are true to ourselves in this way, we are better able to be honest with the people around us. We are less likely to just tell people what they want to hear or try to cover up things about ourselves of which we feel ashamed. Instead, we can be honest about who we are and what we want in a relationship.

Communicate, communicate, and communicate. Frequent, honest communication builds trust. Poor communication is one of the key reasons marriages, work relationships and other relationships fall apart. Communicate clearly and when someone is confused about your communication, be patient and take time to help them understand.

Also, try and give proper feedback, either through words or body language. Feedback is one of the important components of communication that we often undermine. It helps the other party to be sure you are listening and you understand the instructions or their feelings.

Say what you are going to do and then do what you say! Make your actions match your words. Don't give room for people to start doubting what you say all the time. Say what you mean in a clear and straightforward manner and be consistent.

Always do the right thing. We trust those who live, walk and work with integrity. When you don't do the right thing, admit it. Be transparent, authentic and willing to share your mistakes and faults. When you are vulnerable and have nothing to hide, you radiate trust.

Value long term relationships more than short term success. Avoid making money your priority in any relationship; it breaks trust. Value people and relationships more because they will, in turn, help you in making money.

Be open to feedback. Rather than argue every small

detail, we should look for the kernel of truth in what our partner tells us. It's important not to be defensive, reactive, or punishing for feedback. If we get victimized or fall apart when we hear criticism, then we emotionally manipulate people, and encourage them to sugarcoat or even deceive us in the future. Having a person who feels comfortable to open up to us is the best-case scenario for having an honest relationship, in which we can both nurture and develop ourselves.

Avoid passing an insincere compliment, as this is one of the quickest ways to lose rapport and trust with someone. Don't flatter or try to pull legs in passing your compliments.

Ask open-ended questions. Stay open to new ideas and be ready to learn. Ask for clarification when need be. Giving the information back to the sender in your own words is a great way to show you were listening and to demonstrate your understanding. People trust others who take the time to listen.

Avoid exaggeration or showing off. You do not need to make people believe who you are not; you will eventually lose their trust when they get to know the real you.

Admit you don't know something or made a mistake. Everybody makes mistakes and that is why we are human. Do not try to cover up for your mistakes when they are no longer coverable. Admit them and make necessary corrections.

To build trust as a leader in the workplace, lead by example, and show your people that you trust others.

Be transparent. Do not try to pretend, outsmart or play dirty tricks on people; they will not trust you again the day they get to know. Uphold accountability. Don't manipulate - it is possible to use the ideas on this list with the intention to manipulate. Don't do it because it won't end well. It never does. Don't lie - one small lie can destroy a mountain of trust.

Don't fidget. Be aware of your body movements. Minimize your leg shakes, body shifts and hand fidgets. It's hard to trust someone who seems nervous or anxious. Don't also use a" fake voice" by using a British or American accent that you are not familiar with, especially when you are meeting a new person; it might send the wrong signal. Just be yourself

Be accessible. When people know they can get access to you, it builds trust because they can hold you accountable. People who I can't reach always seem less trustworthy to me. Do not create an atmosphere of fear around you.

Have a high self-esteem. Be comfortable with who you are. Don't try so hard to impress; it makes you look wishy-washy. Be careful about the other warning signs of low self-esteem that we have discussed earlier.

Don't abuse privileges. As you gain more trust, you'll be given more privileges. Don't abuse those privileges; stay loyal to them.

Keep secrets. If anybody tells you something confidential, keep it to yourself unless it violates your moral and ethical standards.

Avoid the blame game, take responsibility. When things go wrong, don't point fingers. Empower yourself by taking responsibility and then determining what you're going to do next. Don't waste the present thinking about the past that can't be changed. A person that doesn't blame quickly gains the trust of others.

And don't over-explain. When you over-explain, you're trying to remove yourself from being responsible. This is one of the best ways to lose someone's trust.

Don't gossip. Don't gossip about others. There is a saying: "don't tell me about them because you will tell them about me". if you talk badly about others behind them, you will not only lose your respect, they will not trust you again; and the people who came to tell you about another person will also tell those people about you. So, avoid gossiping; it spoils reputation.

Trust others first. People treat you the way you treat them. Give trust first if you want to get trust. Say this after me, "You can't give what you don't have and you can't get what you don't give."

Develop your emotional intelligence. We have discussed this in chapter 7.

CHAPTER 6
HANDLING CRITICISM

"Criticism is something you can easily avoid by saying nothing, doing nothing, and being nothing." —Aristotle

Criticism is the practice of judging the merits and faults of something. It is an evaluative or corrective exercise that can occur in any area of human life. When you criticize someone, you are condemning or disapproving of them. Naturally, they are less than happy about that as a general rule, and will try to defend themselves, a perfectly understandable reaction. Criticism implies that you are in a superior position to the person being criticized. People have a tendency to resent anything that makes them feel as if they are losing freedom.

How people go about criticizing can vary a great deal. We have:

1. Self criticism
2. Negative criticism/Destructive criticism
3. Positive criticism/Constructive criticism

SELF-CRITICISM

Self-criticism is an idea of fault in one's belief, actions, behavior or school of thought. It requires a great flexibility of mind because it requires a person to be able to call into question their own behavior and thinking, without believing that is "naturally" the way they are or that they "can never be wrong".

It requires being able to step outside oneself and seeing oneself from a different perspective and willing to search for, recognize and accept objections against one's own behavior; accepting that one is wrong or could be wrong.

Actually, some people have "blind spots" in their awareness, such that they are simply unable to see a part of themselves for what it is, except others point it out to them. Such people should not be blamed but they should rather be open enough for people to constructively criticize them and be ready to look into it when their attention is drawn to it.

Self-criticism is an essential component of learning, even though it can be difficult, most times. Just by acknowledging you get it wrong can be very embarrassing and distressing, especially if you have personally invested a lot in the wrong idea. People can be very resistant to admit that they are wrong about something they did or say wrong.

While others might see it as a sign of weakness, the self-critic might no longer have the same confidence or may become vulnerable to attack ("ohhhh you got it wrong, so why should I take you seriously?"). But the beauty of it is that it improves one's style, changes one's behavior and helps to adjust to a new situation.

It is important you recognize your personal errors as such, so that something can be done about it, rather than covering your mistakes and making more mistakes.

While most people regard self-criticism as healthy, as a sign of good character, and as necessary for learning, excessive or enforced self-criticism is regarded as unhealthy. Thus, it is possible to be "too hard on oneself", leading to self-destructive behavior.

The ultimate self-criticism can be a final self-attack through depression, which can eventually lead to deliberate suicide. Suicidal persons are willing to give up their right to exist, because they no longer believe their life is worth living.

NEGATIVE CRITICISM

This is raising an objection to something; showing that it is wrong, false, mistaken, or disreputable. It is the disapproval of something or disagreement on something by emphasizing its downside.

Most times, negative or destructive criticism is done with the purpose of attacking a person, by pointing out that their point of view has no validity at all, or lacks any merit.

This type of criticism is regarded as undesirable nuisance, a threat, or as completely unjustifiable. Its effect is destructive, instead of a positive effect, just like an allegation or an accusation.

Pointing out others' fault in itself is not bad, but when it is proposed in a particular context, it can be very dangerous. It is termed as destructive because, for example, an argument or debate can get out of control and everybody is at war with everybody else. In that way, it can be said that the criticism has been overdone. Even in homes, it can cause psychological harm to children, which can result in lower level of self-esteem, social acceptance and behavioral conduct.

POSITIVE CRITICISM

A positive criticism is well-meant or well-intentioned, without the aim of pulling down or rubbishing another person's words, actions or efforts. The criticism will serve a purpose that is constructive by drawing the attention of the person concerned to the good or positive aspect of something that is being ignored, disregarded or overlooked.

A constructive criticism shows that making the criticism is not necessarily deemed wrong, and its purpose is respected. It is often a suggestion for improvement (how things could be better done or more acceptable) after carefully highlighting the faults.

It is often considered that those who find fault with something should also offer an option for putting it right and that is what constructive criticism is meant to do - to provide a better approach and orientation.

After all said and done, it is important to know that criticism is part of life. It cannot be avoided if we really want to live and not just exist - although taking criticism can be a difficult thing; after all, nobody likes to be told they are wrong.

Criticism is a form of communication that helps get feedback on what you are doing, either personally or professionally. It forces you to think about how you work and can guide you away from bad practices.

I remember, in one of my ACCA classes, one day, the lecturer asked a question and a guy was trying to answer it. After few minutes, I stood up and said "No, you are not right." Everyone stared at me and the lecturer asked the guy to keep quiet, for me to say my own answer that I felt was right. You know what? My answers were also wrong (how nasty that can be!). The lecturer simply pounced on me. He told me never to shut other people down when they are giving their own opinion, whether they are right or wrong. I felt equally bad and ashamed that I had just been embarrassed, but the truth is, even though the lecturer's reaction was kind of harsh, I knew I needed to hear it!

Don't interrupt. When you interrupt, you are telling everyone that what you have to say is more important than what anyone else has to say. And who knows whether you are even wrong, just like me.

How to criticize yourself and others

- Try to be objective and not biased in your opinion.
- Be soft on yourself (for self-criticism); it is just good you have done the right thing by criticizing yourself. Do not be too harsh on yourself while doing that; calm down and move on.
- Be soft on others as well. When trying to criticize them, choose your words carefully. Remember, they are human like you and have feelings.
- Never rubbish their words or effort by pointing out only the faults in it; also try to mention the few good things about their idea.

- Do not try to tell them how you can do it better than they have done; rather, suggest a better way or ways of doing it.

- Use positive language and suggest a solution.

HOW TO HANDLE CRITICISM

- Don't take it personally, not even when the person is trying to be constructive with it; calm down.

- Don't get too used to praises. Criticism helps to recondition us to see things in less black-and-white terms; and with this, there's no limit to how far we can go!

- Understand that criticism cannot be avoided. Most times, it is meant to help you grow. Do not be afraid to be judged; don't take everything as condemnation.

- Understand that criticism doesn't always come gently.

- Criticism gives you the chance to teach people how to treat you. If someone delivers it poorly, you can take this opportunity to tell them, "I think you make some valid points, but I would receive them better if you didn't raise your voice."

- Do not try to be too defensive; there are some words you need to hear.

- You need to understand that you cannot control what

other people will say to you or say about you, but you can control how you internalize it, react to it, and learn from it, if only you can release it and move on.

- Criticism will help for your personal growth and emotional maturity. It will improve your interpersonal human relationships.

- Learn to receive false criticism (feedback that has no constructive value) without losing your confidence.

- Learn to move on after criticism, even if it hurts badly; imperfection is part of being human.

- If you improve how you operate after receiving criticism, this will save time and energy in the future.

- Your critics give you an opportunity to challenge any people-pleasing tendencies. Relationships based on a constant need for approval can be draining for everyone involved.

- Criticism presents an opportunity to choose peace over conflict. When criticized, our instinct may be to fight, creating unnecessary drama but be conscious that people around you generally want to help you, and not necessarily judge you.

- Be objective, try to take a honest look at yourself and your weaknesses; you can grow if you are willing to try.

CHAPTER 7
SELF-LOVE, SELF-ESTEEM AND SELF-CONFIDENCE

If I do not love myself, who will?

Before anybody can love you, you need to first love yourself. I once used a display picture that said "I love my life" and a colleague asked me if it was possible for someone not to love his or her life. My answer is yes!

Self-love is an unconditional feeling of love, appreciation and acceptance for yourself. It comes without the thoughts of "I am not good enough", "I don't deserve it", or "I hate myself". It is a shift of mindset because you don't logically understand it but rather feel it that, no matter what you do, you will always love yourself with the same strength – despite your flaws, mistakes or horrible past.

Self-love involves forgiving yourself of past mistakes. When we harm someone, it is normal and healthy to feel bad about it, to experience regret and to wish we could take it back or do something to make the person feel better. What isn't healthy is to continually beat ourselves up for our offense and to determine we are a bad person because of it. The first experience is generally thought of as guilt, while the second is considered to be shame. I believe that self-forgiveness is the most powerful step you can take to rid yourself of debilitating shame. If you love someone and can forgive them when they offend you, why won't you be able to forgive yourself? Research has shown that people who have a strong sense of guilt understand others' thoughts and feelings better.

SITUATIONS THAT CAN MAKE YOU NOT TO LOVE YOURSELF

- When you get scolded by your boss
- When somebody is mean to you
- When you are mean to someone
- When you could not help a loved one
- When you act on your anger
- When you put on weight
- When you make a mistake at work

- When you eat some unhealthy food
- When you skip your work-out session
- When you lie to somebody
- When you make someone cry
- When you feel lazy

In all these moments, do you still care towards yourself?

HOW TO LOVE YOURSELF

At the start of each new day, remind yourself: "I am talented. I am creative. I am greatly favored by God. I am equipped. I am well able. I will see my dreams come to pass." Declare those statements by faith and before long, you will begin to see them in reality.

Love is a feeling that is nurtured to growth. The first thing to do is to be aware of how you treat yourself. Self-love isn't about what you tell yourself to make yourself feel better; it is about what you do to make yourself better. It is most especially about the hard work we put in to achieve our dreams - the hustle and the resilient efforts. You need not remind yourself that you love yourself because you have already proved it with your actions. Self-love is not an affirmation; it is an action. Saying you love someone and actually loving them are not the same.

What do you do when you love someone? Think of your parent, a lover or your best friend. Do you get them gifts? Do you take them out on a date? Do you pay for them? Do you spend quality time together? Do exactly same to yourself. Do whatever makes you happy, without hurting anyone. Take yourself out for a nice dinner. Treat yourself like a child. Pamper yourself. The moment you envision yourself as a child, you'll notice that the harsh judgment melts away. It's that simple!

Avoid comparing yourself with other people or being in competition with anybody. You are your own competitor; you have to compete with yourself every single day to get the best version of yourself and self-love makes you feel the best of yourself. You can emulate the good things about others, but do not make their life a standard for yours. Everybody has a unique identity from God and comparing yourself with them only makes your life miserable.

Do not allow anybody pull you down with their words or action; and, remember, nobody can drag you down without your permission. Be careful with whom you associate, especially when you feel emotionally vulnerable - because negative people can steal the dream right out of your heart!

If you work and earn a living and you don't spend on yourself and all you think about is other people, then you don't love yourself. When you work, try and enjoy your money by giving yourself some treat; after all, it is those who do not know how much you work for this money that will spend it when you die. Yes, be prudent in your spending but then treat yourself nicely, because it is still yourself.

- Take photographs (taking pictures is my favorite thing for selflove!)
- Visit the museum
- Cook something healthy
- Drink a green smoothie
- Read your favorite book (and yes, it can be that love story you love)
- Watch a romantic comedy
- Buy yourself a nice dress
- Let go of your past quickly
- Get a manicure
- Go to spa
- Dance (and you can perfectly go crazy in your house, I do that a lot)
- Listen to your favorite music
- Play with animals

- Stay in nature
- Go for a walk
- Do nothing (yep! – just sit, or lie down and do absolutely nothing).

SELF-ESTEEM

Self-love is the foundation of self-esteem, it has to do with how you perceive or value yourself. If you do not place a price on yourself, you can be maltreated by people because they will really not know your worth.

Low self-esteem makes you dislike yourself, blame yourself, unable to recognize your strength, unable to make decision or assert yourself. Feeling hopeless and depression may eventually set in. It makes you feel worthless or not good enough. Low self-esteem can be stressful, especially if you put excessive pressure on yourself to be a certain way.

How to improve your self-esteem

- Avoid negative self-talk, you may be unconsciously putting yourself down.
- Connect with people who love you, and spend more time with them.
- Talk to your loved ones when you feel you need help.

- Remind yourself of the things you have done right, and give yourself a pat on the back.

- Learn to be assertive. Learn to say "NO". Set boundaries and take control of your own decisions.

- Set yourself a challenge, find something you like doing and do more of it

- Worry less about what other people think about you. Most times, you cannot control it. Remind yourself that you don't have to be perfect at it to enjoy yourself.

- Celebrate your success, no matter how little they may look.

- Accept compliments.

- Take care of yourself. If you have low self-worth, it can be difficult to find the motivation to take care of your physical health. Sleep well, eat well and exercise your body.

- Do not hesitate to get support if things get too much - peer support, parental support, or go for a professional therapy.

- Focus on your positives. Do not dwell too much on your negatives; it will only keep drawing you back.

- Write down a big goal and post it on your mirror or desk. This can be remarkable.

SELF-CONFIDENCE

Self-confidence is the belief in oneself and abilities. It describes an internal state, made up of what we think and feel about ourselves. This state is changeable, according to the situation we are currently in and our responses to events going on around us.

Self-confidence is extremely important in almost every aspect of our lives as it is an essential part of humanity; yet some people struggle with it. Sadly, people who lack it may find it difficult to become successful. Your level of self-confidence can show in many ways: your behavior, your body language, how you speak, what you say, and so on.

Confidence and self-esteem are terms which are often used interchangeably, although there is an over-lap, there are also subtle differences. Self-confidence can refer to how we feel about ourselves and our abilities, whereas self-esteem refers directly to whether or not we appreciate and value ourselves. We may have been discouraged from being boastful but a healthy amount of self-liking and self-approval is necessary if we are to have the confidence to meet life's challenges and participate as fully as we wish to in whatever makes life enjoyable and rewarding for us. In a sense, we could say that having healthy self-esteem leads to being self-confident.

People with self-confidence generally like themselves.

They are willing to take risks to achieve their personal and professional goals, and think positively about the future. Someone who lacks self-confidence, however, is less likely to feel that they can achieve their goals. They tend to have a negative perspective about themselves and what they hope to gain in life. The good news is that self-confidence is something you can improve!

Building self-confidence requires you to cultivate a positive attitude about yourself and your social interactions, while also learning to deal with any negative emotions that arise and practicing greater self-care. You should learn to set goals and take risks, as well, since meeting challenges can further improve your self-confidence.

Two main things contribute to self-confidence: self-love and self-esteem.

Self-love + self-esteem = self-confidence

There is a thin line between self-confidence and arrogance. While many think self-confidence is arrogance, it is not. Self-confidence is being the best version of yourself (just like we try to update an app or an operating system, which is to bring the best version of what exists) without feeling you are the best in the world or universe. Immediately you start feeling you are the best in the world, then it turns to arrogance.

Self-confidence is keeping your heart open to learn from people around you, bearing in mind that everybody has so much to offer, if only arrogance will not stop you from learning from them. Even though it is hard to learn from people that are equal to us because of envy, pride, ego and insecurity, we can start learning from people who are higher (since you don't have a choice than to humbly listen and submit because they are in authority).

Self-confidence is not arrogance but rather giving yourself the assurance you can dare it, you can do it. And you can get better by opening your mind to learn and accept criticism for improvement.

It is important to be aware of "over-confidence" by not over-stretching yourself. And remember, you cannot gain self-confidence by pulling others down; it will only destroy your personality.

HOW TO BUILD YOUR SELF-CONFIDENCE

Building your self-confidence will be more of how much you love yourself and value yourself (self-esteem).

The list below will assist you to build a strong self-confidence

- Do not focus on your negative thoughts. Identify them and turn them to positives. For instance, instead of "I can't do that; I will surely fail", tell yourself, "I can do it."

- Eliminate all reminders of your negativity. Spend more time with people who love you and do away with people that pull you down or reminds you of your horrible past

- Identify your talents. Give yourself the permission to take pride in them.

- Take pride in yourself.

- Accept compliments gracefully. Take it to heart and respond positively (saying "thank you" and smiling). It works well.

- Look in the mirror and smile to yourself. Tell yourself how good you look.

- Be comfortable with fear; when you are able to confront what you fear, you will gain self-confidence and you will feel the boost immediately!

- Stop comparing yourself with others; you may lack confidence because you're convinced that everyone else has it better than you do. However, at the end of the day, it only matters if you're happy by your own standards.

- Be patient with yourself. Gaining self-confidence does not happen overnight. You might try something new and not meet your goals. If possible, see what lessons are there. Not meeting your goals the first time is an opportunity to learn more about yourself.

Self-confidence needs to be nurtured and grown, a bit at a time.

- Recognize your insecurities. This could be anything from acne, to regrets, friends at school, or a past traumatic or negative experience. Whatever is making you feel unworthy, ashamed or inferior, identify it, give it a name, and write it down. You can then tear or burn these written pieces to start feeling positive on those points.

- Bounce back from your mistakes. Remember that no one is perfect. Even the most confident people have insecurities. Don't let one wrong turn make you think you don't have what it takes to achieve your dreams.

- Avoid perfectionism; it paralyzes you and keeps you from accomplishing your goals. If you feel like everything has to be done perfectly, then you'll never be truly happy with yourself or your circumstances. Instead, work on learning to be proud of a job well done instead of wanting everything to be absolutely perfect.

- Practice gratitude. Often at the root of insecurity and lack of confidence is a feeling of not having enough of something. By acknowledging and appreciating what you do have, you can combat the feeling of being incomplete and dissatisfied.

- Take care of yourself. Put care into your appearance;

dress well. Looking good is a big self-confidence booster for me; it makes me feel good about myself. After all, it doesn't cost so much to look good, once you do not pass your boundary. If you want to feel better about who you are and how you look, then take care of yourself by showering daily, brushing your teeth, wearing clothes that fit you and your body type, and making sure that you've taken time with your appearance. This doesn't mean that superficial looks or style will make you feel more confident, but making an effort to mind your looks tells you that you're worth caring about. Someone once said, "it is not what you wear, it is how you wear it." You do not have to have plenty money or "break the bank" to look good, simple clothes that are relatively cheap and a good dress sense will make you look great as well.

- Eat well, sleep well and exercise regularly.

- Set goals, embrace the unknown and take risks.

- Address your perceived areas for improvement. Don't be too hard on yourself by trying to change absolutely everything. Start with just one or two aspects of yourself that you would like to change, and take it from there.

- Seek to help others. When you know you're kind to the people around you, and are making a positive difference in other people's lives you will know that you are a positive force in the world - it boost self-confidence.

When I was in the university, teaching my classmates gave me this kind of satisfaction and joy. The more I taught, the more I knew more of that course or the more it made me discover that I had not known enough and it also boosted my self-confidence.

Self-confidence is not arrogance; it is simply saying, "No, I'm not settling here. I'm going to keep pressing forward." or "I've come too far to stop now. I may be knocked down, but I'm not knocked out. I'm going to get back up again. I know I'm a victor, not a victim."

CHAPTER 8
A BRIEF INSIGHT INTO EMOTIONAL INTELLIGENCE (EQ)

We probably all know someone who has the ability not only to listen in a caring way but also a master at managing his or her emotions. This person most likely has a high level of emotional intelligence (EQ). Emotional intelligence is the ability to identify, use, understand, and manage emotions to optimize your communications, regulate your emotional reaction, acknowledge others' emotions, and defuse conflict. Improving your EQ can help to optimize the manner you interact with people in the workplace and outside.

The smartest people are not the most successful or have the most fulfilled life. You probably know people who are academically brilliant and yet are socially inept and unsuccessful at work or in their personal relationships. I hope you also understand that there is a difference between being brilliant academically and being intelligent. You can know all the books in the whole world and still not be smart or intelligent; and you can graduate with a C grade and still be the best of staff in a workplace. It's all about IQ and EQ.

One of the bosses I worked with once said, "it is not enough for you to work hard, you also need to work smart." Here is a short story to illustrate this (You might have come across this story before on social media).

Ezra and Thomas joined a company together a few months after their graduation from university. After a few years of work, their manager promoted Ezra to a position of Senior Sales Manager, but Thomas remained in his entry level Junior Sales Officer position.

Thomas developed a sense of jealousy and disgruntlement, but continued working anyway. One day, Thomas felt that he could not work with Ezra anymore. He wrote his resignation letter, but before he submitted it to the manager, he complained that management did not value hard working staff, but promoted only the favored!

The manager knew that Ezra worked very hard for the years he had spent at the company, even harder than Thomas, and therefore deserved the promotion. So, in order to help Thomas to realize this, the manager gave Thomas a task.

"Go and find out if anyone is selling water melons in town." Thomas returned and said, "Yes there is someone!" The manager asked, "How much per kg?" Thomas drove back to town to ask and then returned to inform the manager, "they are N1000 per kg!" The manager told Thomas, "I will give Ezra the same task that I gave you. Please pay close attention to his response!"

So the manager said to Ezra, in the presence of Thomas; "Go and find out if anyone is selling water melons in town." Ezra went to find out and on his return he said: "Sir, there is only one person selling water melons in the whole town. The cost is N500 for each water melon and N300 for a half melon. He sells them at N1000 per kg when sliced. He has in his stock 993 melons, each one weighing about 1.5kg.

"He has a farm and can supply us with melons for the next four months at a rate of 102 melons per day at N450 per melon; this includes delivery.

"The melons appear fresh and red with good quality, and they taste better than the ones we sold last year.

"He has his own slicing machine and is willing to slice for us free of charge.

"We need to strike a deal with him before 10 am tomorrow and we will be sure of beating last year's profits in melons by over N2, 300,000. This will contribute positively to our overall performance, as it will add a minimum of

8.78% to our current overall sales target.

"I have put this information down in writing and is available on spreadsheet. Please let me know if you need it as I can send it to you in fifteen minutes."

Thomas was very impressed and realized the difference between himself and Ezra. He decided not to resign but to learn from Ezra.

You won't be rewarded for doing what you're meant to do; you only get a salary for that! YOU'RE ONLY REWARDEDFOR GOING THE EXTRA MILE; performing beyond expectations.

To be successful in life, you must be observant, proactive and willing to do more, think more, have a more holistic perspective and go beyond the call of duty. I guess Ezra is the consummate supply chain professional.

Emotional intelligence is also known as emotional quotient (EQ). Daniel Goleman popularized the notion in his book published in 1995. He explains emotional intelligence as the ability of people to recognize their emotions and that of other people around them and manage it. Emotional intelligence has now become a very important aspect of humanity, as it is an influencer of personal and career growth. The ability to understand, control and utilize your emotions is crucial to success in work, relationships, family matters and personal health (physical and mental).

Studies have shown that people with high EQ have greater mental health, perform better on the job and have great leadership skills. EQ is not only important for career success; emotional intelligence impacts many different aspects of your daily life, such as the way you behave and the way you interact with others. If you have a high level of emotional intelligence, you'll find it easier to build stronger relationship with other people and achieve your own personal goals.

For most people, emotional intelligence (EQ) is more important than one's intelligence (IQ) in attaining success in their lives and careers. As individuals, our success and the success of our professions today depend on our ability to read other people's signals and react appropriately to them. Therefore, each of us must develop the mature emotional intelligence skills required to better understand, empathize and negotiate with other people — particularly as the economy has become more global. Otherwise, success will elude us in our lives and careers.

"Your EQ is the level of your ability to understand other people, what motivates them and how to work cooperatively with them," says Howard Gardner, the influential Harvard theorist.

EQ AND IQ

Neither is "more" important or "less" important but in the professional world, EQ has gained a great deal of popularity, and many studies have shown that EQ has a significant impact on job performance, interview skills, first impressions, salesmanship, as well as other aspects of business commonly associated with a rising star in the workplace.

In recent times, many employers now test EQ, rather than the conventional recruitment process that only tests the IQ of the applicants. EQ is different from IQ, and having only a high IQ can no longer fetch and retain a job for you. How well you do in your life and career is determined by both. IQ alone is not enough; EQ also matters. In fact, psychologists generally agree that among the ingredients for success, IQ counts for roughly 10% (at best 25%); the rest depends on everything else — including EQ.

A study of Harvard graduates in business, law, medicine and teaching showed a negative or zero correlation between an IQ indicator (entrance exam scores) and subsequent career success.

Also, in order for leaders and managers to attract and retain staff who are 'EQ savvy', they need to engage and explore EQ for themselves. And in doing so, they will acquire a symbiotic emotional quotient assessment tool and knowledge platform – used to measure an individual's adequacy in areas such as social responsibility, self-expression, empathy and decision making – to recruit, induct and develop their workforce. This will ultimately enable an organization's employees to meet and exceed the challenges faced within an ever-changing economic and industrial landscape.

An IQ test will measure how someone learns, understands and apply information in different settings. This is critical to everything in our lives, including our careers, our fundamental behaviors, driving a car, reading a book, and everything in between. Clearly, having a higher IQ can help advance your academic and professional career, and perform the necessary tasks of daily life. However, that isn't the whole story…

EQ is equally as important as IQ. EQ test measures how people learn, understand and apply emotional knowledge. It reflects how someone can understand their own and others' emotions, to differentiate between them, and to use that knowledge to guide your actions and behaviors. Emotional intelligence (EQ) is extremely important for human beings, because we are emotional beings!

These five areas define one's emotional intelligence: self-awareness, self-regulation, empathy, social skills and motivation.

If you have high emotional intelligence, you are able to recognize your own emotional state and the emotional states of others, and engage with people in a way that draws them to you. You can use this understanding of emotions to relate better with other people, form healthier relationships, achieve greater success at work, and live a more fulfilling life

While it has been discovered that IQ can change, as opposed to long-standing beliefs, it can still be difficult to improve our IQ as we age. However, EQ is much more flexible, and can be improved through concerted and conscious efforts at self-improvement.

Some researchers suggest that EQ forms the foundation of all of our interactions and impulses, including the learning process, thus affecting our IQ and cognitive development. However, others oppose that EQ is overrated and has a limited effect on your overall success in life. Consider it this way, having a high IQ might be a good predictor of a career path or industry, but your EQ score will determine how well you will function in that position (e.g. teamwork, leadership, etc.).

Instead of battling with superiority between EQ and IQ in an endless personality duel, recognize the value of both skill sets, improve them whenever possible, and enjoy the benefits that a powerful EQ/IQ combination can bring!

4 COMPONENTS OF EMOTIONAL INTELLIGENCE

1. **Self-Awareness/Self-Regulation/Self-Management.** This enables you to understand your emotions without letting your feelings rule you; and keeping them under control, using rationality to guide your behavior and thoughts, instead of instinct. Knowing your area of strengths and weaknesses and being able to work on them so as to perform better. Most of us are so busy with the daily grind that we rarely take a step back and think about how we're responding to situations that we come across.

The other source of self-awareness is recognizing how others respond to us. This is often challenging because we tend to see what we want to see. And we tend to avoid the uncomfortable action of asking others for feedback. To grow in your self-awareness, consider building time for reflection into your day. Also consider getting into the routine of collecting specific feedback from people who will be honest and whose ideas you value.

A large study that compiled thousands of data points found that leaders who sought out negative feedback were much more self-aware and effective than those who sought out positive feedback. People who self-regulate typically don't allow themselves to become too angry or jealous, and they don't make impulsive, careless decisions. They think before they act.

This component also includes your transparency, adaptability, achievement, and optimism. A key factor is whether you react or respond to situations.

Answer these questions:

- When you get an irritating email, do you write back right away?
- Do you sometimes find yourself regretting how you handled yourself, wishing that you had been more calm and poised?
- Do you lose patience or rush others?

If you said yes to any of these questions, you may be in the habit of reacting rather than responding. When you react, you do what comes naturally, which is going with the emotional part of your brain. When you respond, you act against what is natural, which is why it is difficult. You engage the rational part of your brain and select the best response.

2. Self-Regulation. You often have little control over when you experience emotions. You can, however, have some say in how long an emotion will last by using a number of techniques to alleviate negative emotions, such as anger, worry, anxiety, or depression. Those who can manage their emotions perform better because they are able to think clearly. Managing emotions does not mean suppressing or denying them because all these emotions are normal and may not be avoided at times but understanding them and using that understanding to deal with situations productively is what self-regulation is all about.

A few of these techniques include recasting a situation in a more positive light, taking a long walk and meditating (or praying). These will help to practice self-regulation more

Self-regulation involves:

- Self-control
- Managing disruptive impulses
- Trustworthiness
- Maintaining standards of honesty and integrity
- Conscientiousness
- Taking responsibility for your own performance
- Adaptability
- Handling change with flexibility
- Innovation
- Being open to new ideas

3. Empathy. This is the ability to recognize your emotional wants and needs, and the concerns of other people (that is, putting yourself in other people's shoes). People with empathy are good at recognizing the feelings of others, even when those feelings may not be obvious. Empathic people are usually excellent at managing relationships, listening and relating to others. They avoid stereotyping and judging too quickly, and they live their lives in a very open, honest way.

The ability to recognize how people feel is important for success in your life and career. The more skillful you are at discerning the feelings behind others' signals, the better you can control the signals you send them. An empathetic person excels at:

- Service orientation. Anticipating, recognizing and meeting clients' needs.

- Developing others. Sensing what others need to progress and bolstering their abilities.

- Leveraging diversity. Cultivating opportunities through diverse people.

- Political awareness. Reading a group's emotional currents and power relationships.

- Understanding others. Discerning the feelings behind the needs and wants of others.

4. Social skills. This is knowing how to develop and maintain good relationships, communicate clearly, inspire and influence others, work well in a team, and manage conflict. People with good social skills help others to develop and shine rather than focusing on their own success alone. The development of good interpersonal skills is tantamount to success in your life and career. In today's always-connected world, everyone has immediate access to technical knowledge. Thus, "people skills" are even more important now because you must possess a high EQ to better understand, empathize and negotiate with others in a global economy. Among the most useful skills are:

- Influence. Wielding effective persuasion tactics.

- Communication. Sending clear messages.

- Leadership. Inspiring and guiding groups and people.

- Change catalyst. Initiating or managing change.

- Conflict management. Understanding, negotiating and resolving disagreements.

- Building bonds. Nurturing instrumental relationships.

- Collaboration and cooperation. Working with others toward shared goals.

- Team capabilities. Creating group synergy in pursuing collective goals.

- Motivation. People with a high degree of emotional intelligence are usually motivated. They're willing to defer immediate results for long-term success. They're highly productive, love a challenge, and are very effective in whatever they do. To motivate yourself for any achievement requires clear goals and a positive attitude. Although you may have a predisposition to either a positive or a negative attitude, you can, with effort and practice, learn to think more positively. If you catch negative thoughts as they occur, you can reframe them in more positive terms — which will help you achieve your goals. Motivation is made up of:

- Achievement drive. This means you are constantly striving to improve or to meet a standard of excellence.
- Commitment. Aligning with the goals of the group or organization.
- Initiative. Readying yourself to act on opportunities.
- Optimism. Pursuing goals persistently despite obstacles and setbacks.

HOW TO IMPROVE YOUR EMOTIONAL INTELLIGENCE

- Be conscious of how you react to people; do not rush into judgment before you know the fact. Do not stereotype. Look honestly at how you think or react to other people.

- Try to put yourself in others' place and be more open, accepting their perspectives and needs.

- Practice humility. You can say that you know what you did, and you can be quietly confident about it. Give others a chance to shine – put the focus on them, and don't worry too much about getting praise for yourself.

- Do a self-evaluation. Identify your weaknesses and be able to accept that you are not perfect. Be ready to work on those areas to be a better person.

- Examine how you react to stressful situations. Do not be very upset every time; pause and reflect on issues before you respond. The ability to stay calm in difficult situations is highly valued in the business world and outside it. Keep your emotions under control when things go wrong.

- Take responsibility for your actions. If you hurt someone's feelings or did something wrong, try to apologize. Don't ignore what you did or avoid the person. Do not blame other people and be angry at them even when it is not their fault. People are usually more willing to forgive and forget if you make an honest attempt to make things right.

- Check how your actions will affect others before you take those actions. If your decision will impact others, put yourself in their place. How will they feel if you do this? Would you want that experience? If you must take the action, how can you help others deal with the effects?

- Practice deep breathing and other relaxing exercises to keep a clear mind.

- Learn what triggers are and how they can impact your emotions. It can be challenging to identify what exactly our triggers are, but this process of getting to know and understand them can help us heal, and learn how to cope better in response. But why do we all have triggers? In short, because we were all children once. When we were growing up, we inevitably experienced pain or suffering that we could not acknowledge and/or deal with sufficiently at the time. So, as adults, we typically become triggered by experiences that are reminiscent of these old painful feelings. As a result, we typically turn to a habitual or addictive way of trying to manage the painful feelings.

Once you know your triggers, you can consider their origins. So what are your triggers? What do you do to manage the painful feelings when they are triggered? Do you face your triggers head-on, or attempt to avoid the pain?

- Get a coach or engage in a coaching partnership to help you work on and improve your skills gaps.

- Ask for constructive feedback from others to enable growth in knowledge and competence.

- Undertake an emotional intelligence assessment and a one-to-one feedback session to gain real insight into your EQ profile.

As you've probably discovered, emotional intelligence can be a key to success in your life – especially in your career. The ability to manage people and relationships is very important in all leaders. So, developing and using your emotional intelligence can be a good way to show others the leader inside of you.

CHAPTER 9
THE MAGIC WORDS

I know you would have been wondering by now what I mean by the "magic words". We have a lot of them but for the purpose of this book, our attention will be focused on these three: "thank you", "please" and "I'm sorry". They are words we come about, day in day out, but most of us have not fully understood the power in them. They are necessary to maintain healthy relationships in every field of life. How difficult is it to show appreciation or remorse even in the simplest form in words?

These three words - please, I'm sorry and thank you - are often called magic words because they make a person feel important, pacify tempers, strengthen bonds and, at times, mend strained relationships. Only a thoughtful, polite and grateful person uses them often.

As human beings, we all want to feel appreciated, loved and respected. By treating people around us in a proper manner, we show them the courtesy and respect they expect from us. In addition to this, these magic words also make us feel better about ourselves.

Teach your children how to use these words with you as a parent in the house, and among their siblings. Use these words for them as well and encourage them to use the words outside among their friends. By the time they grow up, the habit would have already become a part of them.

The use of magic words with your children at home can reduce tension and help raise helpful and grateful adults. Teach your children about good manners from an early age. If you do, they'll always be respectful.

Children to Parents/Friends:

"Thank you, Mummy, for attending the Christmas carol in my school today."

"I am sorry, Juliana, for not helping you fix your broken watch as promised."

"Please, Daddy, can you help me pick my dress from the laundry shop on your way back home this evening?"

It makes you as a parent feel not being taken for granted by your children.

We must understand that all relations are based on the policy of give and take! Children are usually on the receiving end, but by showing their gratitude when their requirements are met, asking for something in a polite manner and apologizing when they have done something wrong or have hurt someone, is their way of paying back the efforts of their elders.

Parents to Children:

"Olajide, can you please bring my handbag?"

"I am sorry for shouting at you the other time, Alex."

"Thank you, Elizabeth, for making this nice meal for the family today."

It will help boost their self-esteem, give them a sense of belongingness and make them feel happy.

Please:

This is a kind of request to be able to enter into the life of someone else with respect and care. We must learn to ask: may I do this? Are you happy if we do this? Asking permission is knowing how to enter somebody else's life with courtesy. Sometimes, we charge in, as if we were wearing heavy walking boots and stomp around the life of a partner. True love does not impose itself with hardness and aggression. And today in our families and in the world, there are often violence and arrogance because there is a need for far more courtesy.

We must understand that there is a very thin line between

a demand and a request, but often we fail to see the difference. When we say "please", it shows respect and consideration.

Often in school, we need help from a friend or a classmate. We may need to borrow a book which we forgot to keep in our bag, or require something as trivial as a pencil, which we have misplaced. Sometimes, a friend is better at a subject, in which we are lagging behind and we want him to explain it to us during a free period. At the workplace, you might need someone to pick up your document for you from the printer when you notice that he or she heading there.

These favors may seem small to us. If we take them for granted and do not consider it important to say "please" before asking for something, it tells a lot about our personality

Sorry:

In our lives, we make mistakes, we all do! And this is why we need to be able to use this simple word, "I'm sorry". Let us learn to recognize our mistakes and to apologize. "I'm sorry I raised my voice"; "I'm sorry I didn't stop to say 'hi'"; "I'm sorry I was late"; "I'm Sorry, if I was quiet this morning"; "I'm sorry, if I spoke too much without listening"; "I'm sorry, I forgot" and so on.

Arguments between husband and wife are normal, but never end the day without making peace. By the next day, the feelings you kept inside would have become colder and harder.

Saying "Sorry" for something we have done wrong, whether intentionally or unintentionally, may be a bit hard on our ego, as admitting a mistake is often difficult. But once we realize how important it is to apologize in a required situation and how far it goes in strengthening a relationship, it will be effortless to swallow our pride and the word will come easily to us.

Suppose somebody pushes you as you are descending the stairs after school is over. In trying to balance yourself, you bump into a friend just ahead of you and he falls. You may either mumble something like "It was not my fault" and move on; or you may stop and say "I am so sorry, but someone pushed me and I lost my balance", then pull your friend back to his feet and help him gather his bag, water bottle and lunch box. Which approach do you think is correct and will make your friend feel better?

A person who says sorry when they are not sure is called wise.

A person who says sorry when he is right is called Matured.

A person who says sorry even when he is not right is called honest.

Gratitude (Thank You):

Someone once told me that she says thank you to all her service providers, from her hair stylist to her car engineer, fashion designer and even the gate-keeper. Isn't that amazing - even when they get paid for these services they render! But the truth is that if that hair stylist of yours broke her appointment with you at the last minute and you could not rock that nice hair you had been dreaming of to that party, how would you feel? I bet you, I might not go for that party again or I would go but not be my cheerful self. That would have definitely ruined my day, I must tell you!

Research has shown that the way a person treats a restaurant staff reveals a lot about their character. Same goes for the way vendor treats their customers. Do not treat any customer/client as if you are doing them a favor. For God's sake, you will be paid for this! And even at that, after they patronize you, learn to say a heartfelt "thank you" because - think about it - they could have patronized another person (that can even do it better than you).

Saying "thank you" to people is an appreciation that they have decided to be kind to you against all other options they might have. And learn to never say your "thank you" too late because it might have lost its value by then.

It is necessary to know how to say "thank you" genuinely, when we receive a good gesture from people around us, regardless of whether they are paid for it or not. Who knows, they may have other good options.

Showing gratitude to God is important but showing gratitude to people around us is equally important. Saying "thank you" is a simple and often overlooked way to show someone how much they mean to you. The gesture is made even more special when you've taken the time to include a small gift and a handwritten nice message in order to express your gratitude.

Principles of Gratitude

- Recognize the wonderful things that have been done for you - the loving parents, the amazing friend, the affectionate spouses, those wonderful teachers, the intriguing boss, that amazing spiritual personality and so on - by saying THANK YOU!

  Our life is a sum total of these wonderful things that they have done to our lives. We have a lot of affluent and influential people. What the world really need are transformed individuals who can show gratitude for the good deeds they have received so far.

- Remember the good that has been done to you. These days we tend to forget things badly, especially the good ones; but we are quick to remember the bad ones. Gratitude is about remembering the good people have done to us. We are what we are in our lives today because of the sacrifices people made for us because strength comes by lifting others. Remembering makes us mean the "thank you" we say because, many times, we say these words without meaning them.

- Reciprocate. Isn't it going to be incredible if we start trying to pay back the good gestures we receive! It is not just enough to recognize or remember good deeds; it is equally important to reciprocate all the good that has been done to us. Gratitude is not just the words ("thank you") or feelings; it is the action we put in by doing something good to those that have done something good to us by assisting them in their dreams too.

You can show gratitude to nature and God for value for life, value for food – gratitude for all we have received and all we have become by reciprocating to the society through supporting the community out there – that is, giving to the needy, charity organizations and campaigns, the widows, fire victims, flood victims, homeless children. You can even pick a needy child in your neighborhood and sponsor his or her education. There are, indeed, many ways you can give back to the society.

Remember,

A taker can eat well but a giver will sleep well.

A taker can have a great time but givers will have a great life.

In the act of giving there is satisfaction, joy, and a sense of fulfillment.

Life cannot be balanced without giving. In the mathematics of life, the more you divide the more it multiplies. This means the more you give, the more you have. This incredible equation is what makes life amazing. Note this, in the act of giving, sharing and caring, there is satisfaction.

CHAPTER 10
LIVING A SUCCESSFUL LIFE

We have various perceptions of what success is. In fact, the definition of success is subjective, because we have different views and beliefs on what success is.

We all want success. We want to be successful and feel successful. We chase money, fame, power, education, relationships and a thousand other things without ever stopping to ask one essential question: What actually is success?

What success means is a personal view and the yardstick to measure it can only be set by individuals. If you cannot answer what you think success means in your own context, you will end up climbing the wrong ladder and pursue someone else's version of success. And you might get to the top, only to discover you had climbed the wrong mountain, achieving your goals only to realize they were the wrong ones. It's a disaster only few people are able to recover from.

"If you don't design your own life plan, chances are you'll fall into someone else's plan. And guess what they have planned for you? Not much."

However, it is easy to assume that success means obtaining a specific object, such as a job or social status, and to believe that if we get that thing, we'll be successful. But some of the greatest successes were birthed from the worst failures. Winston Churchill said, "Success is not final, failure is not fatal. It is the courage to continue that counts."

WHAT SUCCESS ISN'T

Before we can pursue success, we need to understand what success isn't. If you spend just a few minutes on social media, you'll realize the so many narrow definitions people hold about success. They think it's about building wealth, having the perfect relationship, launching a billion-dollar business, or amassing a large number of social media followers or Facebook friends. And a lot of times, they attach famous people to their image of success.

None of these things or people is wrong, but being like them doesn't necessarily make you successful. Many people have fought and struggled to the top, only to feel miserable and burned out once they get there. They're unhappy because they pursued the wrong definition of success—one that didn't match their values. In order to lead the life that you desire, you must set your own goals and idea of success according to what you want — not what television or your parents want. This is all about you, your life, and idea of success.

Throughout childhood and early adulthood, we learn various ideas of success from our parents, teachers and friends. Everyone has their own agenda and idea of who and what we should be. Although it's OK to value the opinions and hopes of others, we shouldn't necessarily adopt them as our own. No one can impose their version of success on us. No one can tell us what it means to live the good life.

If we rest our definition of success on one or two achievements, there's a good chance we'll be disappointed. Success is creating meaningful, purposeful and fulfilling lives and being able to make an impact and a difference in the lives of other people. To me, success means making my dream of a renowned public speaker come to reality (because that is where my passion lies), living a good moral life that makes my words binding on me, being a happy person, impacting other people's lives positively, leaving a good landmark in the lives of people I meet in life and being a good influence and example for my children.

That is my own definition of success - not how many cars I have or how many estates I own or how many countries I have visited or how many children I have or how many nice pictures I have on social media to show off or how many educational qualification I have. What is yours?

THE CONCEPT OF HAPPINESS

The simple, yet profound, truth is that what makes me happy doesn't make someone else happy, and vice versa. Some people find out that helping people brings them the most joy, and therefore success looks like a life given to others. Some realize that building a business or product brings them happiness. For some, pursuing their passion gives them happiness. While some prefer isolation, others prefer constant activity.

We are surrounded by a materialistic culture and to get to experience first-hand kind of "happiness" it brings when we obtain a specific title or object. You may even feel it from time to time, like buying the new iPhone or basking in the scent of a fresh new car. It's not necessarily bad to have these things, but many times, the reasons we crave these things are a bit misconstrued. Some of them are needs and not basically luxury. True happiness cannot be found in material things; true happiness comes from within.

In trying to enhance and increase your standard of

living, please do not compromise on those principles that also improve the standard of your life. It is not the standard of your living that makes you happy or makes you successful; it is the standard of your life.

We forget to give attention to those things that truly makes us happy, wealth and material things have utility value, not happiness value. Happiness is not the amount of money you have but the people in your life who help you create wonderful memories.

HOW TO ACHIEVE SUCCESS

- Ask yourself: what is success and how do I achieve it? If we fail to define success for ourselves and try to pursue someone else's path, we'll end up frustrated, unhappy and ultimately feeling deeply unsuccessful. Bruce Lee said, "Always be yourself, express yourself, have faith in yourself; do not go out and look for a successful personality and duplicate it."

- Once you remove the veil of what success really means to you, only then can you start achieving it daily and on your own expectations. The more you strive to be better than yesterday, the more success you will feel because progress, at times, can be felt.

- Chances are, if it makes you happy and requires you to use your skills and effort, then you probably should be doing it every day. The new phone or car, flying first class, using an expensive wristwatch — those are just temporary rewards; they won't last. Do what makes you happy the most.

- To free yourself from the limitations of what others perceive as success is a tremendous opportunity to define life on your own terms. You learn to stop chasing things that simply don't matter — but at one point you thought they did — and instead, you start to focus on the things that help you differentiate progress from procrastination.

- The fruitless emotions of anger, jealousy and resentment should play no part in the attainment of your endeavors and the ability to succeed; those are just distractions.

- Don't wait to start living like this. You can start today. As a matter of fact, you should start today, because continuously living everyday with expectations that are not of your own is a day that is not truly yours.

- Really sit down — even write it out if you have to — and define what success is to you. You can create both short-term and long-term goals. My short-term goals consist of writing daily, accomplishing my tasks, and being of service to others. My long-term goals would be finishing my book, writing more books that can help humanity, building my readership on my blog, and seeing others achieve their goals over time.

- Nobody likes a person who complains all the time. If you look around you, you'll see many people who have been dealt a bad hand, but are making the best of things. I use to have a boss who was always complaining. He never saw anything good about the company or the management; so embittered and negative.
- Don't blame others for your problems
- Don't make excuses
- Don't be overly sensitive
- Don't be a drama queen

Do you want to live a successful life?

1. Surround yourself with supportive people.

Three things can change your life: friends, books and your thoughts. Choose them wisely. Avoid naysayers and party-poopers who don't have purpose. People have a huge impact on your life. "You are the average of the five people you spend the most time with," says American entrepreneur and motivational speaker, Jim Rohn. With this in mind, you should think about the people you're spending time with the same way you think about what you eat and how you're exercising. Some people can be parasites. They suck out your happiness, energy and, maybe, some of your tangible resources as well. You can put spending time with them in the same category as eating pizza on the couch.

2. Have a positive mindset.

You are what you think all day long. If you have nothing but negative thoughts racing through your ahead, then that's what you are going to get. So, try shifting to a more positive outlook on life. You will be surprised to see that whatever you wished for will start to manifest itself around you. Stop thinking about what happened in the past, or worry about what may happen in the future. Live in the moment and learn to savor each one. "Whether you think you can, or you think you can't—you're right," says Henry Ford

3. Treat others how they want to be treated.

You might end up getting in trouble if you try treating others how you want to be treated, instead of how they would like you to treat them. For instance, if you are not a phone person, you might not call your friend because you assume that they feel the same way you do, which may not be the case.

Try to be sensitive to the needs of others, and occasionally going out of your way to do something for them. Try not to judge. Be generous; try to do something nice for somebody on a regular basis.

4. Use everything in moderation.

This is something I live by - be it work, socializing, family commitments, overeating, shopping, or watching too much TV—it helps with every single thing. Embrace the philosophy of "having enough". There's no need to go to extremes; so exercise common sense and learn to curb any obsessive behavior.

The day I told my kids that "too much of everything is bad", it became a song for them. I think it sounds so funny to their ears and it's like they had not heard about it before. And they started asking, "Mum, is too much of eating bad?" I said "Yes". "Is too much of sleeping bad? I said "yes" is too much of reading bad? They thought I will say "No" because I have always force them to go and take their books and read, I said "yes" too and they started laughing loud.

- Spend less money than you make

- Watch your diet

- Watch less TV

- Use social media less

- Be fashion conscious less

- Don't be too serious

- Don't be too strict

- Don't be too loose
- Don't be unnecessarily awkward.
- Yes, too much of everything is bad – EVERYTHING!

REFERENCES

Daniel Goleman 1995, Emotional intelligence

Joel Osteen 2004, Becoming a better you

Seven secrets of a confident woman by Joyce Meyer

Anna Kudak 2010, What happy women do

www.bravebelle.com

www.tinybuddha.com

www.mindtools.com

www.dawn.com

www.albertocei.com

www.success.com

www.mindorg.uk

www.wikihow.com

www.cdnpsychologytoday.com

www.moneycrashers.com

www.seenandheardus.com

www.cosma.org

www.mdedlibrary.org

www.witcheri.blogspot.cz

www.scienceabc.com

www.healthcaremarketingassociation.com

www.lifehack.org

www.stottclinicalhypnotherapy.com.au

www.en.wikipedia.org

www.mentorsassociation.citadel.edu

ABOUT THE AUTHOR

Omobabinrin Adeola Osideko M.sc ACCA is a Chartered Accountant and also a Certified Public speaker (Expert rating certification), a young lady who has passion for public speaking especially in the area of behavioral sciences. She works with African development bank as a Finance personnel.

Adeola is a steady rising public speaker who started some 3 years ago and she has been continuously developing her skills and passion in making humanity better through her public speaking career. She has been opportune to attend few number of trainings, seminar and conferences on Public speaking, emotional intelligence and many more both as a student and as a speaker.

Her observation about some of the behavioral issues we have in our society has inspired her to write this book in order to address these areas and make our society a better and safer place to live.

She is married with children.